Soul Contracts

"Danielle MacKinnon helps you not only gain an understanding about the foundation of your Soul Contracts, she also expertly guides you to become the master of your own destiny. Follow her compelling, heart-inspiring system and discover how to fully embrace your pure potential."

—**Rikka Zimmerman**, speaker, author, and creator of Adventure In Oneness

"Author Danielle MacKinnon tackles a complex topic (Soul Contracts) and skillfully transforms it into a study that's understandable and palatable to the human psyche. The information she provides will give you the tools needed to identify and release the internal limitations that prevent you from living a meaningful, purposeful, and joyful life. This book is not only a good read, it is life changing."

—**Carol Ritberger PhD**, author of *Healing Happens with Your Help*

"This book is a must-have for anyone wanting to transform their life! Danielle MacKinnon writes a warm, compassionate, user-friendly guide to understanding your Soul Contracts. Learn what they are and how they work, and gain valuable hands-on tools to master your Soul Contracts and live the life you have always wanted!"

—**John Holland**, psychic medium and author of *Spirit Whisperer*

"Brilliant! This book was obviously divinely inspired—
I couldn't put it down. It's not just a book on Soul Contracts
but rather a 'manual for life' with our whole Soul System clearly
defined. For anyone who wants to understand why in spite of all
effort, chaos envelops your life—read this book and learn to release
negativity at the soul level. I promise, it will change your life!"

—**Cindy Kubica**, speaker, author,
and host of Energized Living Today

"If you're seeking to get to the root of what's blocking you in life
in order to create lasting improvements, *Soul Contracts* reveals a
step-by-step system. A handbook for Soul-level change, this book
teaches you how to recognize, release, and remove what is holding
you back from your dreams and desires so that you never have to
repeat the same patterns again. A brilliant new book for people
seeking the next level of spiritual insight and growth."

—**Bob Olson**, BestPsychicMediums.com,
BestPsychicDirectory.com, and AfterlifeTV.com

"In *Soul Contracts*, the celebrated intuitive Danielle MacKinnon
introduces a new and powerful healing system that can remove
chronic barriers to your inner peace and joy. Let her take you on
a journey of self-discovery and transformation to reclaim the
wonders of your Soul's profound wisdom."

—**Brian L. Weiss, MD**, author of
Many Lives, Many Masters

Soul Contracts

FIND HARMONY AND UNLOCK YOUR BRILLIANCE

DANIELLE MacKinnon

ATRIA PAPERBACK
New York London Toronto Sydney New Delhi

 BEYOND WORDS
Hillsboro, Oregon

ATRIA PAPERBACK
A Division of Simon & Schuster, Inc.
1230 Avenue of the Americas
New York, NY 10020

BEYOND WORDS
20827 N.W. Cornell Road, Suite 500
Hillsboro, Oregon 97124-9808
503-531-8700 / 503-531-8773 fax
www.beyondword.com

Managing editor: Lindsay S. Brown
Editors: Gretchen Stelter, Emily Han
Copyeditor: Claire Rudy Foster
Proofreader: Deborah Jayne
Design: Devon Smith
Composition: William H. Brunson Typography Services

First Atria Paperback/Beyond Words trade paperback edition June 2014

ATRIA PAPERBACK and colophon are trademarks of Simon & Schuster, Inc.

Beyond Words Publishing is an imprint of Simon & Schuster, Inc., and the Beyond Words logo is a registered trademark of Beyond Words Publishing, Inc.

For information about special discounts for bulk purchases, please contact Simon & Schuster Special Sales at 1-866-506-1949 or business@simonandschuster.com.

The Simon & Schuster Speakers Bureau can bring authors to your live event.
For more information or to book an event, contact the Simon & Schuster Speakers Bureau at 1-866-248-3049 or visit our website at www.simonspeakers.com.

Manufactured in the United States of America

10 9 8 7 6 5 4 3 2 1

Library of Congress Cataloging-in-Publication Data

MacKinnon, Danielle.
    Soul contracts : find harmony and unlock your brilliance / Danielle MacKinnon. — First Atria Paperback/Beyond Words trade paperback edition.
        pages cm
    1. Spiritualism.   2. Self-realization.   I. Title.
    BF1275.S44M23   2014
    131—dc23

                                                                        2013050765

ISBN 978-1-58270-456-2
ISBN 978-1-4767-3905-2 (ebook)

The corporate mission of Beyond Words Publishing, Inc.: *Inspire to Integrity*

To my husband, Kevin.
To my son, Cole.
I love you both with all my heart!

Contents

Contents

Preface

One Saturday, I walked out of the gym, tired, depressed, and troubled. My puppy Bella was sick, and no one was able to figure out why. As I scanned the parking lot for my car, I saw my friend Cindy. She always had a huge smile, and no matter my mood, her happiness was contagious. It felt like a sign: she appeared at the moment I really needed a smile.

As we chatted in the parking lot, I mentioned how upset I was. Bella had been at the vet's for the past four nights. Cindy knew how much I love animals. She patted me on the shoulder as I sniffled. My heart broke at the idea of Bella lying in a crate in pain. Suddenly, Cindy brightened. "Wait!" she said. "Why don't you take her to a pet psychic?"

Neither of us could predict the massive ripple effect her words would create in my life. Since I was a child, I had been supersensitive, with a strong connection to the animal kingdom. I remember telling my mother that I knew what each of my thirty-two caterpillars was thinking. I sensed how my hamster was feeling. I also knew what other people were thinking or feeling. Before I went into a room, I knew if the person in it was angry or happy. My mother didn't know anything about intuition, energy, or psychic abilities—so I was labeled "oversensitive." She took me to doctors, psychologists, and others to try to help me feel comfortable with myself.

But the problem wasn't being uncomfortable with *myself*. I wasn't comfortable with the world. My intuitive senses absorbed so much, but I had no one to share it with. I ended up thinking I was weird and different. If I expressed an interest in anything like psychics or intuition, my mother steered me in the other direction, believing she was protecting me. But if I had faced my sensitivities head on, my pain might have been immediately relieved!

So, when Cindy mentioned a pet psychic, it was like hearing a buzzer. I was finally free to investigate the world of intuition and psychic sensing. I rushed home and immediately made an appointment.

The next morning—antsy, nervous, and excited—my husband, Kevin, and I traveled north with Bella to a hotel in Nashua, New Hampshire. I left Kevin in the car with our depressed and pain-ridden dog, and I practically ran into the pet psychic's office. When I met Bruce, I was totally taken aback. He looked *normal*. I wasn't necessarily expecting a turban, rings, and eyeliner, but I thought he might look somehow different, alternative. This psychic looked like a regular guy: a computer programmer, engineer, or data processor.

As I led Bruce out to the parking lot, he asked me not to disclose anything about my situation. My sick, little baby dog sat still in the car. When I opened the door, she didn't bark, try to jump down, or whine. She stared straight at Bruce. At first, I thought she was so silent and contained because she didn't feel well, but as I watched her interact with Bruce, I realized something else was going on.

After a few minutes, Bruce turned to me and said, "She says she's upset."

"I'm sure she's upset. *Why* is she upset?"

"She's upset because she says that you and your husband have been fighting." Pause. "About your mother."

I was floored. He was right—we had been fighting for the past week about when to visit my mother-in-law. We had been traveling so much lately that I never wanted to leave the house again, but Kevin felt differently. Our drawn-out fight had gotten ugly, and we had forgotten what we were really fighting about. Bruce went on to say that the fighting was making Bella anxious. She had gotten into the trashcan and eaten three corncobs because she was upset, but she was about to pass them and would be fine. He said a lot more, and everything he shared rocked me to the core. I could feel something within me shifting.

Until that moment, I had been following the typical path of an MBA. I had a great job in marketing, woke up and went to the gym every morning, spent my day doing project management, got home by six, ate dinner with my husband, watched some TV, and then went to bed. Each day was the same, and I was not happy at all. A piece of my Soul died every time I walked into my office building. My husband and I had talked plenty about moving back to California, relocating to the coast, or downsizing so that I could take time off and write a book, but none of those ideas appealed to us. We were both stumped. What could we do to get happy or at least feel more fulfilled?

When Bruce said the word *mother* to me, that was *it*. A switch flipped deep down in my Soul. In fact, it was a Bump Contract intended to knock me off my feet and set me back onto my true life path. (You'll learn more about Bump Contracts later on.) I knew immediately that I wasn't supposed to be doing project management for someone else's business—I was supposed to be helping people and animals. I realized this other life was completely possible. I accepted that I was psychic and became ready to start using it.

In the next couple of weeks, I took an animal communication class. I got to experience and practice my intuitive abilities. As it turned out, I was really good at this psychic stuff! My overall excitement and passion for life increased. I dreamed about leaving the corporate world to help animals; within a month of the class, I had opened up my own part-time animal communication business. I wasn't ready to fully give up the comfort of my "real job" and saw clients in the evening and on weekends.

Although running my new company was easy, I couldn't really enjoy it. I was petrified that someone I knew might find out what I was doing. I was tossing aside mainstream values for something more risky; there weren't many people who would understand or support me. I was certainly afraid of what my mother would say. After I sent out my first newsletter (to an email list of twenty-two people!), my mother called me on the phone. She said, "Danielle, you're not sending that to people who can see it, are you?" Another family member who attended one of my events said, "Dan, I don't know what to tell people that you do." Each step I took toward making my dream come true pulled me further away from the high-end corporate success plans my family had for me.

At first, things went smoothly, as I had imagined they would. After returning home from my office, I worked at animal communication. Most of my appointments with people and their animals were over the phone rather than in person. I spent my time asking animals if they liked their beds, needed more walks, wanted different food, had hurt themselves, and so on. Rapidly, a theme started to emerge from the animals—a grand plan for me. It was all I could do not to resist, close up shop, and run screaming back to the white-collar world.

The first time it happened, I was working with a lovebird and his human, Tom. Tom had come to me because his bird, Larry, had been pulling out his feathers. I began my usual telepathic connection with Larry. I tried asking Larry my standard questions: "Are you sick?" and "Are you allergic to something?" and "Is something in your environment setting you off?" At first, Larry wasn't being clear, and I couldn't understand him. Finally, I heard him say (in my head), "Because of my Soul Contract with Tom." At the time, I didn't know what that meant, although I soon found out. In subsequent sessions, other animals talked to me about their Soul Contracts with their humans. This was a serious endeavor for the animals, as I didn't know anything about Soul Contracts; I thought they might have something to do with Soul Mates (they don't!).

These animals taught me a lot. I learned that they each had pre-birth agreements with their humans to help those people evolve. I learned that animals will sacrifice their comfort, security, bodies, and well-being to assist their human in learning a Soul Lesson. I suspected that not a lot of people knew this yet.

Did I want to learn this? Did I want to become the messenger? It was already a huge deal to go against my family's wishes and become an animal communicator—now I heard a strong message to take my work to the next level. So what did I do? I stalled and whined, hemmed and hawed. I did not want to be the person on the cutting edge, offering new ways of thinking to the world. Why couldn't I just be normal—or at least a regular animal communicator?

But the animals had plans for me. A woman hired me to help with her Chihuahua, Jesus. The dog had been peeing in a plant in the kitchen, and the behavior was causing a big problem. Both of Jesus's humans (a husband and wife) were up in arms about the urine smell, the plant killing, and Jesus's seeming lack of house training.

I had no idea that this six-pound Chihuahua would be the one to make me finally accept my new direction. I connected with him energetically and began with a few questions: "How does your bladder feel?" and "Do you know where to go to the bathroom?" But Jesus's answers weren't really clear. Finally, when I mentioned the plant in the kitchen, Jesus let it all out. He told me that he was very aware of where to pee and where not to pee, but that he had a Soul Contract with his human. He was required to help her learn how to take care of herself. Then he told me that the only time he peed in the plant was when his human's husband was hitting her.

I was floored. This was not what I expected or wanted to hear. In fact, this new information put me in an awkward position; I was embarrassed to say what I knew. I asked Jesus what I should do. He told me to tell her that there were times in the kitchen when the energy got very "hard and loud," and it was only at those times that he would pee inappropriately. He told me to tell her that when she took steps to get herself out of this situation and take care of herself, he would stop peeing in the plant. He also explained how he would pee in the plant less and less as she evolved. I used Jesus's words, and his human heard me. More than that, I finally heard what the animals had been trying to get me to understand.

After that session with Jesus, I threw my hands in the air and surrendered. The animals had led me down an unexpected path, but it was time to let go of my plans. For a little while, it was easy to follow along. A person would come to me with a dog, cat, guinea pig, or other animal; the animal would explain how their problem was related to their human and how to help both of them. I finally began to feel comfortable.

But the journey was just beginning! Soon, my work caught on. Clients came from all over the United States to experience my unique method of connecting with animals. It was very exciting! I loved working with Animal Soul Contracts and now realized that was my purpose on Earth. It felt amazing to finally be in alignment with my calling.

Several months later, I found myself struggling to stay on the animal side of my Animal Soul Contract work. For example, a dog told me that his refusal to eat mirrored his human's bad self-care. The dog asked me to work with his person, to teach him how to take care of himself and find the Soul Contract that was creating this behavior. Or another time, I connected to a horse that wouldn't turn left. He said he was trying to embarrass his human, who was very concerned with what everyone else thought. With my help, the horse's human could break the Soul Contract that held her to needing approval from the outside world.

It was all very confusing. I just wanted to stay in my new comfort zone, but my work didn't make that seem like a possibility. As time went on, I sometimes began a session by connecting with an animal, then ended it working solely with the human. Very quickly, as my experience with Soul Contracts grew, people began booking sessions for themselves, without their pets. My human clients were plagued by Soul Contract blocks and needed intuitive guidance on how to get free.

I slowly accepted my next new direction—interpreting Soul Contracts for animals and humans. After seeing many success stories with my clients, I looked around the self-help industry and noticed that I had become an expert—if not *the* expert—in Soul Contracts. And I wasn't even aiming for that! Thank you, animals!

As a Soul Contract consultant (for humans and animals), my career really began to take off. Psychic medium John Holland came to me for a reading with his dog, Koda. Through this reading, he learned about himself and his own blocked areas—and was so impressed that he included an account of the session in his book *Spirit Whisperer*. Later, psychic investigator Bob Olson added me to his list of Best Psychic Mediums. I began to work with human and animal clients all over the world, focusing on Soul Contracts and helping people to become the best they can be.

Since embracing Soul Contracts as my work, my experiential education (what I've learned through my sessions) has continued. My readings incorporate even more about contracts and their under-lying energies. I am so grateful for that ah-ha moment with Bella that led me to my true calling, and it's my wish to share this knowledge with others who can benefit—like you.

Introduction

Many unseen and unconscious energies influence you every day. They can cause you to behave a certain way, think a certain thought, or believe certain ideas about yourself—these energies are your Soul Contracts, and they are part of your Soul System. All these ways of thinking, feeling, and believing take away from your ability to discover who you really are. They prevent you from living the life you want to live, having the relationships you so deeply desire, finding the success you're craving, and more. They also provide a beautiful, detailed road map for figuring out how to get where you want to be. The things that are blocking you from your achievements are actually showing you how to free yourself.

Imagine that you're driving down the highway. You pass a sign that cautions "Road Work Ahead." Now that you've been warned, you're able to prepare for the challenge ahead, figure out your options, and make any needed adjustments. You can choose to drive around the construction, find an alternate road, or even turn around and drive in the other direction. Once you know that there is a block (and what it is), it's much easier to manage.

The problem arises, however, when we do not interpret the warning signs correctly or miss them entirely. For example, imagine you had your head turned the other way as you drove by the sign. Perhaps you interpreted the sign to mean the road is impassable, when it really isn't. Many people today read the sign and think, *Well, that's the way it is. There is a block up ahead and I just have to accept it. That's the way it goes and that's just who I am.* That's the real problem—when we start assuming we are broken, stuck, unworthy, and unlovable. Many people unknowingly sabotage themselves by accepting their blocks as part of themselves.

Nobody but you will get you through your blocks. The barrier ahead is there for you, and only you, to go through because it represents a lesson your Soul needs to learn in this lifetime. So how do you identify and interpret these road signs? You can begin by learning about your Soul System.

The Benefits of Working with Your Soul System

In this book, I'll call these different energies your Soul Contracts, Seed Thoughts, Discordant Emotions, and Root Belief Systems. They make up your Soul System, and I'll define them more comprehensively in chapter 1. These energies manifest as challenges—hidden but pervasive blocks that stop you from reaching a goal or push you to have negative feelings about yourself. These energies are actually shortcuts to learning life lessons and achieving your goals—but first you need to master and rework your Soul System. Rather than getting upset when a block shows up in your life, try to think of it this way: You now have inside information about what has been holding you back from your happiness, peace, and success.

As you can imagine, great results can come from mastering your Soul System; however, the work can appear daunting, since you must address all levels—energetic, mental, emotional, physical, and spiritual—in order to experience the greatest release and forward momentum. These blocks can prevent you from just about anything, from cutting your hair, to getting along with your dog! They are also the key to awe-inspiring results. Through this work, I've seen people finally become free: leave unhealthy relationships, start their own business, stand up to their mother, write a book, go back to school, find the love of their life, believe in themselves, find their voice, lose weight, become rich, love their body, and more.

There is no limit to what you can do when you finally accept how beautiful, whole, pure, and good you really are—no matter what decisions you've made in your life so far. As you begin to master your Soul System, you will begin to let go of the blocks that keep you trapped in the land of *he said, she said* and *I can't* and *I don't know*. You will travel toward energy, spirit, and oneness—where beauty, perfection, experience, and love are all that exist. The results of this work are often tangible—you might make $100,000 in four months or meet the love of your life—but they are also intangible. You might feel a trust in yourself that you've never felt before or develop a connection with yourself that you didn't know could exist. Whatever you are looking for, you can receive it, but you will most likely receive so much more.

In committing to take on this Soul-level work, you will be minimizing your fears, worries, frustrations, and other disempowering emotions so that you can experience unconditional love, the beauty of being human, and the Light of who you are.

Why Other Methods Haven't Worked

Many self-help techniques don't help in this type of work for one of two reasons. First, they ask you to consider yourself broken; they offer you a tool to "fix" yourself. But that perspective is far from the truth. In fact, you are absolutely perfect! The influencing energies within your Soul have kept you from accessing your completeness and perfection, but this book will assist you in rediscovering that.

Second, many self-help techniques ask you to work at a superficial, purely behavioral level, rather than the Soul level. The changes you make in your life at that level do not create long-lasting forward movement. Since you're only working to act differently, you have to monitor your new behavior all the time. But when you change your energy at the Soul level, the old challenge will stop existing. You won't have to make sure you are speaking up or that you are putting yourself first—it will happen automatically. This book will help you delve deeply into the level of the Soul where true changes can take place.

There are also a lot of techniques out there that say they can clear your blocks instantaneously or that a new tool can immediately change your life for the better. Working at the Soul level is not about quick fixes, instantly feeling better, or letting someone else give you the answers. Instead, it is about learning what you were born to know, which will clear away all that is blocking you from seeing, feeling, believing, and experiencing your true perfection.

We have a natural predilection to protect ourselves, so we don't want to revisit anything that was emotionally difficult. No one likes to look at the pain they've been hiding within themselves, but uncovering that pain is part of exploring your Soul System. Your journey will take you deeper than you've ever been before. You may not like the emotions that come up, but the benefits far outweigh the very temporary discomfort. The pain you've been avoiding is what has been creating all these blocks in your life. You must address that hidden energy in order to move toward experiencing your own brilliance. You must do your own inner work to discover your light.

Many of my clients have told me that even though they had been working on overcoming their blocks for years, they still hadn't achieved the results they were looking for. The difference between most other types of work and mastering your Soul System is looking at the scary parts of yourself. We won't avoid it. Trust that it will get better as you work through your Soul Contracts. You will begin enjoying amazing freedom from the blocks that were holding you back.

Look at any previous work (whether you had wonderful results or not) as the foundation you needed to prepare to do this work today. Consider that work with gratitude and positive thoughts. Additionally, as you understand and master the various components of your Soul System, your earlier self-work with other teachers, books, and classes may become more helpful and may make more sense than before.

The Five Steps to a Healthy Soul System

We will be going into these steps in great detail in the upcoming chapters. In the first four chapters, we'll define Soul Contracts (and the other parts of your Soul System) and give you a foundation to build on. Next, we'll jump into getting you unblocked.

Step 1: Build Your Foundation
In this step, you will learn how to make your personal energy strong and clear. You will develop the ability to make superior decisions as you move toward a healthy Soul System.

Step 2: Increase Awareness
You'll work on identifying the components of your Soul System that need release—the disempowering Soul Contracts and blocks.

Step 3: Embody the Lesson
In this step, it's all about making different decisions and following new patterns based on what you've learned from your process so far.

Step 4: Establish Mastery
Here, you will see that all of your small, sustainable steps toward embodying the lesson have brought you success on every level.

Step 5: Release
Lastly, you will learn two powerful methods to release your Soul Contracts and Seed Thoughts.

You'll be given exercises, tools, and examples to help ensure that you are successful in your work with each of the steps. Remember, working deeply is not working quickly. You may find that you spend only a few hours on one of the steps, while another one takes you a full week or more. How fully and completely you explore each step will affect how you move through the ones that follow, so take your time! Often, you will unknowingly begin doing the work of your upcoming step. It indicates your readiness.

Terms in This Book

While you won't need to read this book with a dictionary by your side, you will want to keep certain terms in mind. For example, you'll notice that the phrase *100 percent Divine Light* is used throughout this book. In my practice, we work with energies and beings of the highest vibration. To me, the phrase *100 percent Divine Light* indicates that vibration. There are many energies in our world that are not 100 percent Divine Light. Energies that are not 100 percent Divine Light are not purely derived from Source, so they can't connect you to your greatest and highest good. Permitting only 100 percent Divine Light is a simple, wonderful way to filter out any lower vibrational energy that doesn't serve you. Just think of energies of less than 100 percent Divine Light as negativity. No one wants to work with negativity.

There are several instances in this book where I will suggest that you work with your *Guide Team*. Your Guide Team is the group of spiritual beings assigned to you by the Universe. They watch over you, protect you, support you, and give you information, guidance, and assistance whenever you ask for it. Your Guide Team is made of up beings who have never been in a physical body, so it won't include any deceased loved ones. If a Guide Team does not fit your belief system, just substitute whatever you are comfortable with. For example, perhaps you want to call upon God, Source, or angels. Or perhaps you're not really sure how the Universe is organized. In that case, instead of calling on your Guides, take a moment to relax.

When I refer to the *Universe* or *Source*, I'm using a term intended to be broad enough to fit any belief system. Perhaps your belief system includes God, Allah, angels, goddesses, or Guides. It doesn't matter what term you use, since all our work is based on intention. *Universe* is your cue to fill in the word that fits best with your beliefs or whatever term you are most comfortable with.

Another term is *Discordant Emotion*, a negative emotion that is present when you start to lose your connection to your Soul.

In this book, I also refer to past lives. Past lives are an interesting subject; everyone seems to believe something different. When referring to a past life, I am referring to reincarnation, in which a person's Soul is reincarnated over many lifetimes as that Soul works toward enlightenment. Although many of my clients do not believe in past lives or reincarnation, they are still able to work successfully with their Soul Systems. If your beliefs do not include past lives, you can skip those parts of the book.

The only difficult piece of this work is committing to it. Once you start identifying your patterns and working with your blocked energies, you'll find that things begin to click and flow together. Mastering your Soul System is a journey of self-discovery. It's a treasure hunt, where the chest of gold is your own inner brilliance and beauty. So take a moment now to dedicate yourself to exploring your Soul System, and let's begin.

What You Need to Work with Your Soul System

You don't need much to do the work in this book effectively. First, come to the table with an open mind about yourself. The people who experience the greatest success are those who are willing to consider alternative reasons for their challenges. Additionally, this book puts the responsibility for your problems on you, at the Soul level. It's not about blaming yourself; you created these energies one way or another, and since you created them, you're the one who has control over them (and that's a good thing).

Finally, you will want to have a journal or notebook to record your thoughts and feelings while you work the steps to get your Soul System back into balance. There are several exercises where you'll be writing down your ideas. You may find it's easier (and feels safer) if you dedicate one particular journal or notebook to this purpose.

1

The Soul System:
The Foundation for Your Brilliant Life

Your Soul is the beautiful, brilliant, and unconscious energy within you, connected yet amorphous. I imagine it as a big ball of silvery gold light that shines from the core of every human. In a healthy Soul System, your Soul drives your decisions, how you feel about yourself, and how you perceive the world. Through this work, you can regain full access to it, so you can discover your light and live brilliantly.

As you re-access your Soul, you'll come to realize that:

You are safe.
You deserve to be happy.
You are loved.
You can feel satisfied.
You can be stimulated by your life and live with passion.
You can wake up and love your life every day.
You can be abundant, wealthy, and supported.
You are a good, whole, healthy person.

When our Soul Systems are unhealthy, we hide these truths from ourselves, unknowingly denying ourselves real happiness and success. A healthy Soul System comprises three main parts:

1. Your Soul. Your Soul is the essence of your being and the foundation of your existence here on Earth.
2. Your connection to Source—to the Universe. With this connection in place and its pathways cleared, your intuition balances with your logical mind perfectly.
3. The living desire to help you see, feel, hear, breathe, experience, and know the unconditional love that exists within all of us, every day.

There aren't many components in a healthy Soul System because it's not that complicated! Accessing your brilliance is an easy, everyday occurrence in a healthy Soul System. A Soul System becomes unhealthy when it contains at least one Root Belief System. When you have a Root Belief System within your Soul System, your connection to your Soul is blocked. This prevents you from accessing the brilliance of who you really are.

Instead, you'll end up tapping into the untruths within your Root Belief System. A Root Belief System makes it difficult for you to believe in your brilliance. To get your Soul System healthy, you must release the Root Belief Systems within it. These systems cause repeating patterns of unhappiness, failure, sadness, depression, anger, and negativity.

One of the fascinating things about the Soul System is that it's malleable, and it's this malleability that we'll be taking advantage of in this book. You can influence your Soul System consciously and unconsciously through very strong emotions, such as love, fear,

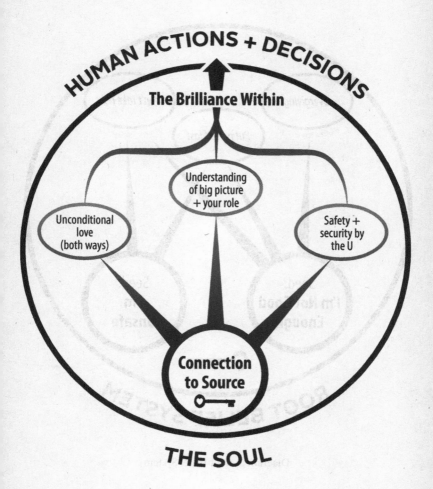

Diagram 1: Healthy Soul System

and insecurity, but you're not going to affect it by deciding to try out the new fad diet or declaring that you're going to quit smoking. These are superficial, everyday occurrences that arise in the moment rather than touch you deeply. Because they happen at a superficial level, they don't affect the Soul.

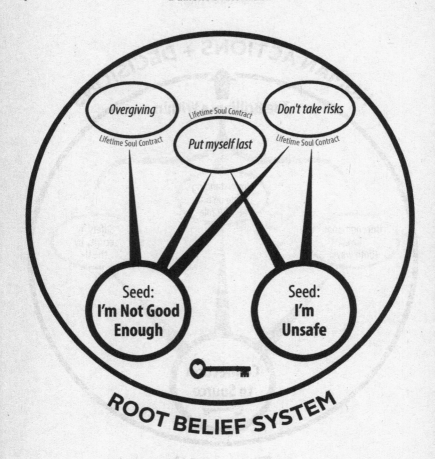

Diagram 2: Root Belief System

Every once in a while, however, an event creates a Discordant Emotion such as fear, desperation, longing, or depression, or a subsequent erroneous belief about yourself, such as being unworthy. Experiences like this can kick off a Soul-level change within, or you might push away these thoughts and emotions because they make you feel less than the brilliant Soul you are. When this occurs, the important piece is not the actual event—it's how and why you decided to push away in that emotional and energetic state. Avoiding or burying those Soul-level emotions leads to the creation of a Root Belief System by planting a Seed Thought.

Seed Thoughts: The Energy on Which Your Soul Contracts Are Anchored

To embody the idea that we can be loved, satisfied, deserving, and completely happy, we must accept our light, our beauty, and our brilliance. So many of us (more likely, *all* of us) have struggled with this idea. We feel hurt by something someone said or didn't say, or did or didn't do. Rather than address it, we ignore or run away from it. For example, as a child, you may have heard your mother say that your sister was "the smart one." She may have told you that you'd never amount to anything. This created pain, but you ignored it and pushed through—you wanted to get on with your life. You didn't stop to explore your reaction or the real reason your mother made this statement. You still suppress these negative feelings rather than taking time to understand them.

When you do this, you are actually burying that idea or thought within your Soul—you are creating a Seed Thought. You essentially take a negative thought about yourself (and the emotions surrounding it) and plant it inside you. Most of us believe that ignoring a negative thought will take away its power, but the truth is that it immediately starts to fester. As the Seed Thought grows, it will undoubtedly influence your life, your decisions, and how you look at life—and yourself. This happens so frequently and so subtly that we don't realize the influence that old thoughts *still* have on us.

To understand how Seed Thoughts work, let's look at four-year-old Sara. Her father is sick and has been hospitalized for two years.

Her mother takes care of him day and night in the hospital. Sara is old enough to understand that her father needs help from her mother, but at the same time, she feels tossed aside and ignored. Her own need for love is not being addressed. Her reaction is to feel bad about herself, disappointed in her mother for the lack of attention, and betrayed by her mother. As a four-year-old, Sara can't confront her mother and say, "You're not taking care of your children! We need love too! You're our mother, and you should be here for us!"

If this happened to Sara as an adult, she would have more choices. She could choose to have a conversation with her mother or seek emotional support from a friend or lover. If Sara had this choice—which is not a choice to ignore the lack of love, but to neutralize it—her experience would result in a memory of a difficult moment instead of buried, negative beliefs.

As a child, Sara does not yet have the strength, world view, or power to rise up against her mother's behavior. She accepts what her mother does, along with the negative emotions (Discordant Emotions) and thoughts that it creates: abandonment, anger, disappointment, sadness, and loneliness. In an effort to stop experiencing that negativity and get through this part of her life, Sara buries those thoughts and emotions within her Soul, creating two Seed Thoughts: *I am not good enough* and *I am not lovable*. In doing this, Sara thinks she is protecting herself from the pain and negativity related to missing her mother. She is right, temporarily. She won't suffer emotional pain in the immediate future, but not too far down the road, those Seed energies will show up again and again.

As Sara's life progresses, she'll feel the effects of those Seed Thoughts and Discordant Emotions. In fact, she'll feel them more acutely than she would have if she had just allowed herself to experience the negativity when it first appeared. This is because Seed

Thoughts (also called shadows, negativity, entities, and more) are powerful energies holding particularly negative vibrations.

Sara's Seed Thoughts will radiate into her world and reflect back to her as experiences, decisions, and thoughts. These beliefs will have a negative vibration that matches the seeds, eventually causing Sara to create Soul Contracts. Sara will also continue to experience events that reinforce the pattern of abandonment, anger, disappointment, loneliness, and sadness—the same Discordant Emotions she felt toward her mother when she was four. Until she learns the lesson underlying her seeds, Sara will never be truly free of this system.

Planting a Seed Thought is like placing a negative, foreign vibration into a system designed to radiate only inner light and brilliance. A healthy Soul System will vibrate with your Soul's beauty, unencumbered by worries, fears, or hate. Negativity does not naturally exist within the Soul System. Each time you plant a Seed Thought, you are not only affecting your Soul System with the negative vibration, but you also are marking a place in your Soul where you must return in order to discover and embody your inner positivity and brilliance.

Your Soul System is your most sensitive instrument and ally. Great white sharks can detect even the smallest amounts of blood in the ocean from three miles away, and your Soul System is infinitely more receptive than that. When you experience pain, your subconscious thinks, *Let's just hide it.* But as soon as that hidden pain enters your Soul, the system begins to align with it. Now each of your movements and thoughts contains the painful vibration of your Seed Thought. For example, if you buried pain related to the idea *I'm not good enough*, guess what? Everything you do from that moment on will reflect your *I'm not good enough* vibration. You are either being influenced by it or reacting to it. For instance, you may have chosen your high school boyfriend because, deep down, you thought you weren't good enough for someone better. Or, if you were rebelling against your Seed Thought, you may have picked him because you wanted to prove that you *were* good enough for someone like him.

That single Seed Thought has wriggled its way into every aspect of your life. It has shaped your personality, chosen your friends, influenced your career, and governed your relationships. As time passed, you lost your connection to the brilliance of your Soul and believed the lie from the Seed Thought.

Buried thoughts and emotions are like drops of water falling onto the surface of a pond. Each creates a ring that ripples outward. That is how Seed Thoughts affect your system. Whether you obey your Seed Thought or resist it, *not being good enough* and *fear of failure* will still be part of every choice and action. Even if you attain every goal, become successful in business or in love, and receive awards, you'll continue to suffer from feelings and thoughts related to the original Seed Thought. The way to get free is to go within; find the hidden, painful Seed energy; learn from it; and release it. Once you do that, you will begin to experience your perfection—something you always had but didn't believe in.

The Seed Thought and the related Discordant Emotions join together as an energetic shield that slips between you and your Soul. The more Seed Thoughts, Discordant Emotions, and Soul Contracts you have in that shield, the harder it is for you to tap into the beauty of your Soul. Instead of experiencing life through your vibrant Soul and feeling happy, whole, secure, and positive, you'll be operating from within that energetic shield. The shield will reinforce your fears, Discordant Emotions, and false beliefs about yourself. You will feel burdened and unhappy because you aren't connected to your Soul.

Additionally, once embedded in your Soul, each seed begins communicating its message to your body, mind, and environment.

You *know* it. The vibration is so subtle that you don't realize you are being driven by anything other than your healthy Soul; however, because like attracts like, you will have many opportunities to re-experience that Seed Thought. The seed attracts experiences into your life that match it. Let's look again at Sara, whose mother wasn't around when she was little. Even though Sara believed she had overcome her emotions of inferiority and thought they would no longer affect her, she was still touched by them every day. She experienced thoughts, emotions, events, and people that were aligned with her Seed Thought. Therefore, Sara continually felt inadequate. Even when she showed the world that she was not just good enough but great, her Seed Thought made it extremely difficult for her to believe she was good enough.

Sara still does not understand why she feels inadequate. She sees herself as a disappointment. These experiences create more negative feelings, until one day, Sara says, "I'm going to prove I'm good enough, no matter what!"

This moment of extreme frustration, which stems from repeatedly experiencing her Seed Thought, is when Sara creates the next piece of her unhealthy Soul System: the Soul Contract. The contract she puts in place says she will do everything in her power to prove she is lovable, *at all costs*. Sara now has a Seed Thought driving her to feel not good enough, plus a Soul Contract, which says that she *must* prove that she *is* good enough, no matter what. You can see how this creates a bigger problem for Sara.

So, a Seed Thought is a thought (or energy) that someone buries within their Soul to avoid dealing with it. As that Seed Thought vibrates within their Soul, it begins to attract matching negative experiences, people, and events. Once this person is fed up with those negative experiences, they will try to take control of the negative energy by making decrees, vows, contracts, and agreements intended to negate the Seed Thought. These are known as Soul Contracts.

Soul Contracts

A Soul Contract comes from a perfect storm—all the elements must come together at the right time. The Seed Thought energy must be strong enough to push you to create a Soul Contract, rather than just make a behavior change. If Sara had been venting to a friend, she couldn't experience the perfect combination of negativity and desperation needed to produce a Soul Contract. It takes a very deep level of anger and frustration, as well as at least one underlying Seed Thought, to create a Soul Contract. After all, the Soul Contract only needs to exist in order to counteract the Seed Thoughts.

A Soul Contract can only be fulfilled by realizing that you cannot satisfy it. It is a dead-end proposition: the best action you can take is to understand why you put it there in the first place. No Soul Contract can help Sara prove to herself that she *is* good enough. She could go to Harvard, get an MBA, make millions of dollars, have a loving husband and children, and still never believe she is good enough—as long as that Soul Contract is anchored in her Soul by her underlying Seed Thoughts. She'll have to fix this from the other direction—by understanding and then addressing what drove her to think she wasn't good enough in the first place. When Sara finally does this, she will be on the road to releasing the block and creating a healthy Soul System.

As you're learning, a Soul Contract indicates an area of your life where you have some deep work to do—a lesson to learn. It points to a place within where you don't believe in your own brilliance. It is a waving flag that shows you where you've lost your connection to your inner light. Soul Contracts stop you, create discomfort, block you, and make you feel scared or less-than in an infinite number of ways. The only way to relieve your discomfort and break through that block is to learn what you aren't getting, realize it, and live it. Then you can move toward happiness, peace, freedom, protection, support, and enlightenment. Once you do, you'll be reconnected to your Soul, purpose, and passion. You'll be able to achieve that which previously seemed impossible—you will finally embody the perfect being of light you really are.

When a Soul Lesson is ignored, Soul Contracts become bigger blocks. You may have several tumultuous and traumatic experiences; their purpose is to draw your attention to a point in your life where you lost the connection to your Soul. These contracts often manifest people or events in your life that create chaos and strife (or love and laughter, depending on the lesson you need to learn). Soul Contracts are pervasive and hidden—until you know how to look for them—and then they become glaringly obvious. They provide deep guidance, secretly compelling you to think and behave certain ways.

Many people think they already know all they can know about their Soul Contracts. They see these blocks as unalterable. In fact, I have run into several people who wanted me to help them accept their Soul Contracts, rather than understand, master, and release them. In my private practice, people often ask if I can release their Soul Contracts immediately, rather than doing the underlying work that would help them identify the Seed Thought behind the situation. I say there is a reason they created the Soul Contract, so they must learn that lesson in order to be free.

Soul Contracts provide a special opening into yourself. Once you understand them, your Soul Contracts allow you to live with all the peace, happiness, abundance, freedom, and passion you've ever wanted.

Root Belief Systems

Years ago, when I first started working with Soul Contracts, I helped my clients discover the main contract that blocked them. We would work together on that particular contract from various points of view until they had released it. A few months later, the clients would return, saying, "I'm struggling again." This puzzled me. As I looked into what was happening, I discovered something: the Seed Thought was just as important as the Soul Contracts—and it was understanding how all of these components came together to create a particular Root Belief System that brought each person the greatest success in the work.

When you created your Soul Contracts, you didn't know you were doing so in order to stop yourself from experiencing your Seed Thoughts. You thought you were just doing whatever it took to feel better. Because people aren't aware of their Seed Thoughts, the problem in creating a Soul Contract is that it doesn't actually accomplish what you want it to—because it doesn't rid you of the seed, it only covers it up temporarily. Soul Contracts make you feel like you have some control—that if you could just do X or achieve Y, or prevent yourself from feeling A or B, you would be fine. So what do most people do when their first Soul Contract doesn't give them the result they wanted? They create more Soul Contracts, all in an effort to stop one Seed Thought from appearing in their life. When you have several Soul Contracts anchored to a Seed Thought, which is surrounded by a few Discordant Emotions, you have created a powerful Root Belief System. (Luckily, this power is erroneous, because it's based on false beliefs!) To be released, you will have to address all the pieces (the Seed Thoughts, Soul Contracts, and Discordant Emotions) of your Root Belief System. But don't worry—you're going to learn how. And it's not that hard!

It can feel overwhelming to do this Soul System work, but as you go deeper, your intuition will assist you. As you tackle one piece, other parts of your Root Belief System will emerge and shift as well. If you find that you have more than one Root Belief System, it does not mean you are worse off than a person with just one. You are not broken! No one is. You've simply made decisions in your past that hid your beauty, belief, and brilliance from yourself—but it's all still in there. You're finally on the path to unlocking it.

An unhealthy Soul System can comprise one or more Root Belief Systems (see diagram 3 on the next page). Each Root Belief System blocks access to your connection to your Soul, making you believe that the only way to feel better or succeed is to obey the Root Belief System. Again, imagine that the Root Belief System is a shield between you and your Soul. Instead of tapping into your Soul when you have an experience, you tap into that root. The unbalanced belief system tells you, "You're not safe, don't do that" or "Wait! You're not good enough to pull that off!" In this book, you will learn how to dissect your Root Belief System, grasp the lesson you need to learn, embody your new knowledge, and release it. The goal is to help you access your inner brilliance.

Sometimes the pieces making up your Soul System are small— lessons that you can learn without a lot of strife—but if you don't learn them, the Root Belief System expands, the Soul Contracts get bigger, and the blocks become more massive. They do this in an effort to force you to start working with your Soul System.

As you master the components of your Root Belief System, your new knowledge will have a different effect on the system as a whole.

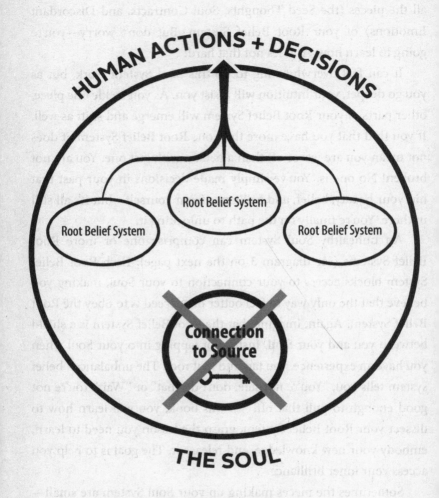

Diagram 3: Unhealthy Soul System

Each block you release will have a positive impact. Once you have released the entire Root Belief System, you'll be able to see the truth about yourself and the brilliance you've been doubting because of those root beliefs. In the end, the only belief system that matters is the one from your Soul, which tells you that you, everyone, and everything are perfect, brilliant, safe, and whole.

Soul Purpose vs. Soul Contract

Your Soul Purpose is not a part of your Soul System, and it's very different from your Soul Contracts. Let's distinguish between the two.

Every human has a pre-birth plan that determines what they are supposed to do in their lifetime. This plan is distinct from a Soul Contract. The Soul Purpose is your main contribution to human consciousness. It may be to teach others to be more kind, work with those who are less fortunate, create a great work of art, or act as a role model in some way. Before you were born, you programmed your Soul Purpose into your being, and until you align with it, you will feel incomplete. Once you begin working toward your purpose, however, people will take notice. When you encounter someone who seems to have a special gift or natural talent, you are seeing their Soul Purpose.

Soul Contracts, on the other hand, are related to lessons that your Soul needs to learn in your lifetime in order to advance spiritually. These Soul Contracts may have been put in place either during your lifetime, in a past lifetime, or even during the pre-birth stage. The big-picture purpose of a Soul Contract is to master its lesson; the big picture of your Soul Purpose is to align with it and let it guide you. Each person has many Soul Contracts in their life. Learning about them can help you become more aligned with your Soul Purpose. Often, a person will have at least one Soul Contract (such as "avoid risks" or "remain invisible in life") that prevents them from discovering their Soul Purpose.

If you want to figure out what your purpose is—the thing that will make you feel wonderful—create a healthy Soul System. Your

Soul Purpose and Soul System can then complement each other beautifully!

Everyone wants to know what their Soul Purpose is—but it's impossible to discover it if you don't believe you are smart, see yourself as successful, or think you are lovable. Each person's Soul Purpose is part of a grand plan—and it takes a healthy Soul System to get there. So let's make your Soul System healthy, and you can start reaping the benefits!

2

The Four Types of Soul Contracts

There are two main categories of Soul Contracts. There is the Lifetime Soul Contract (consisting of past and present life), and there is the Pre-Birth Soul Contract (consisting of relationships, animals, and bumps). Although we'll be focusing on Lifetime Soul Contracts, it's important to have a grasp of the other three types as well, since they play a secondary role in your Root Belief System. Although we won't be working directly with them in this book, understanding how they inform your Soul Lessons will be a great help.

Pre-Birth Soul Contracts

Pre-Birth Soul Contracts are based on the idea that the Soul never dies. It moves between lifetimes and the Source, forever. Many people refer to this movement as reincarnation. Pre-birth refers to the time between lifetimes, prior to the Soul's next incarnation. That is the time when the Pre-Birth Soul Contract is formed.

When the Soul is in a pre-birth, between-lives state, it is in its most high-vibrating form. This is the state of pure, loving, absolute connection. Every Soul continually works upward to reunite with the Source at its own pace. The more inner work we do during our lifetimes, the more we reconnect with our Soul's brilliance between lives.

Pre-Birth Soul Contracts are agreements that occur between two Souls during this pre-birth state. Since this pre-birth state is the highest possible vibration, anything created during this period will be for the Soul's highest good. Your Soul knows exactly which Soul Lessons you will be learning in your upcoming lifetime. If you died in your previous life with several Soul Contracts in place, your Soul knows that you're going to have to work on them in your next life. Your Soul also knows what you have already achieved in terms of universal understanding and enlightenment.

It goes like this: Your Soul approaches another Soul saying, "Hi, John. In my upcoming lifetime, I'm going to work on believing in myself. Would you assist me with this?"

John's Soul says, "Sure, Melissa. In my upcoming lifetime, I'm going to learn to be more independent. Can you help me?"

The agreement between the Souls becomes a contract. At some point in their lives, Melissa and John will meet and begin assisting each other.

Yes, you're reading that right—other Souls purposely enter your life in order to help you learn your Soul Lessons and climb up that vibrational scale toward enlightenment. That includes the boss who drives you nuts because he takes credit for your work; your mother, who claims she supported you every minute of your life but actually abandoned you when you were three; and the clerk who offered to carry your groceries to your car for you. These are all contracts!

Pre-Birth Soul Contracts are energetic agreements in their highest vibrational form. Their only purpose is to help the Soul evolve, learn the lessons it has been struggling with, and move closer to enlightenment. They are contracts we want to understand, master, and live out; this will allow us to evolve and live brilliantly.

A lot of people don't like the idea that their life is predetermined. They feel that Pre-Birth Soul Contracts take away their free will. Free will, however, plays a huge role in Pre-Birth Soul Contracts and in the Soul's ability, once embodied, to master the Soul Contract efficiently and easily. Although your Soul's lessons are preassigned, the path you'll take to accomplishing your work is not predetermined. The way two Souls will create and fulfill a Soul Contract isn't predetermined either; that is based on free will. In our example, it's possible that John's Soul will help Melissa by becoming her lover, but it's equally possible that he will fulfill his Soul Contract by becoming her employee. The only piece of the arrangement that is actually predetermined is that these two Souls will meet and that somehow their interactions will be geared toward helping each other with their particular Soul Lessons.

Your Soul has created millions of Pre-Birth Soul Contracts with other Souls. When you meet someone and feel a *zing*, that's the activation of the contract. Of course, not every person you meet will create that feeling, because every Pre-Birth Soul Contract is different. However, if you consider every person in your life a teacher who can show you something about yourself, you are beautifully on track. This can be difficult, though, when one of those "teachers" is taking credit for your work or is flirting with your boyfriend.

As you can see, working with any of your Soul Contracts helps you evolve on many levels—even the ones you are not aware of.

Relationship Soul Contracts

Relationship Soul Contracts are one type of Pre-Birth Soul Contracts. You have a Relationship Soul Contract with every person you will ever come into contact with. That includes all your family members, your kindergarten teacher, and the driver who gave you the finger as you merged onto the highway. Of course, some agreements play a much larger role in your life than others.

Relationship Soul Contracts are based on the lessons your Soul wants to work on in your current lifetime. In every interaction, you have something to learn. For example, you may have a contract with your mother; she is supposed to help you learn about your own inner beauty, and she might do it by putting you down or by being very beautiful herself. If you consider that every relationship, no matter how big or how small, can point you toward your Soul's inner light, you can perceive the power of your Relationship Soul Contracts.

The current status of a relationship has no bearing on whether there is a Relationship Soul Contract. As I said before, there is a Soul Contract between you and *every other being you come into contact with*. The person can be part of your daily life, someone you only met once, or even someone you see on TV.

Surprisingly, mastering a Relationship Soul Contract is not contingent upon the other person in any way. Your lesson is for you. It's also possible that once you get the lesson, you will no longer need the teacher. Furthermore, the other person doesn't have to get their lesson from you for the Relationship Soul Contract to be fulfilled. The point is to come together to give each other an opportunity to learn a Soul Lesson.

Mastering the lesson in a relationship does not guarantee that the two of you will stay together as a couple, as friends, or in any other way. Doing this work in your Soul System is not easy. It's not fun to think that if you create a healthy behavior, start believing in yourself, or find success, certain people may not fit your new way of living—but it is a fact. Not every person will leave your life as you master each Relationship Soul Contract, but many will. In the long run, having friends, family, colleagues, and others who leave your life because they can't handle the changes you've made will result in the greatest and highest good for everyone involved. But initially, it could really sting. Try to think of it this way: each person who leaves your life as a result of your Soul System work will open up a space for a new person who matches the new vibration you hold.

Working with a Relationship Soul Contract could, and often does, make relationships stronger. I've seen many people create successful, long-lasting relationships out of unhealthy ones because they finally understood what the other person was there to teach them. They learned how to allow that lesson to guide their behavior within the relationship. Relationship Soul Contracts don't bind people together forever, but for some, the connection they create is deep.

Mastering a Relationship Soul Contract is primarily an individual act. The opportunity for the other Soul to learn is present as well, but your partner's mastery is not guaranteed. Sometimes your learning process can occur many years—even decades or lifetimes—after the relationship has ended. Until you are ready to deal with the lesson within that relationship, that Relationship Soul Contract will linger and fester. Most people will compound the problem by creating many more Lifetime Soul Contracts to avoid doing this deep work.

Animal Soul Contracts

Animal Soul Contracts are the second type of Pre-Birth Soul Contracts. These are just like Relationship Soul Contracts, except that they occur between human and animal Souls. Unlike a Relationship Soul Contract, the animal Soul does not ask for anything in return for its help.

Unlike humans, animals have already mastered unconditional love. Animals don't worry that they're too aggressive, too fat, or not smart enough. They don't practice cruelty toward one other because of different belief systems. This is why rescuing an animal can be such a rewarding experience for a person—animals have a capacity for love that is like nothing a human can experience. Animal Souls exist on Earth in order to help humans discover how to evolve toward unconditional love. As you work on your Animal Soul Contract and master the lesson your pet is helping you learn, your pet will receive from you in one of two ways. Either the changes you make directly create a better environment for the animal, or your increasing energy vibration affects the overall vibration of human consciousness in a positive way. The animal works with you toward either outcome.

Yes, this does mean that many animals are sacrificing themselves—their bodies, their physical health, and emotional well-being—in order to help humans learn. Based on the animal abuse still occurring around the world, we have a lot to learn. When humans achieve what the animals are trying to teach us, we will live in harmony with the rest of the planet for each incarnation. The goal of every Animal Soul Contract is helping you and humanity rediscover the brilliance within.

Bump Contracts

Bump Contracts are the third type of Pre-Birth Soul Contracts. They are created by your Soul in the pre-birth state as a kind of plan B.

Preceding each lifetime, your Soul knows that you have specific Soul Lessons you need to learn in order to make your way to a state of pure, unconditional love. Your Soul also knows that the road to enlightenment is fraught with turmoil, resistance, and free will; sometimes, a bit of extra help is necessary. A Bump Contract will only show up in your life if you are avoiding a particular lesson. For example, perhaps you are taking care of your ailing mother, forgetting that you have needs as well. The Bump Contract may appear in your life as a physical illness that demands you pay attention to your own body. Many people get confused by Bump Contracts and call them "punishments from God." People have also inaccurately described Bump Contracts as coincidences completely unrelated to their journey on Earth. They are not negative, random events, as many people who have experienced them can tell you.

Bump Contracts can take many forms in a person's life. They can show up as a cheating spouse, a winning lottery ticket, or even a serious diagnosis. The purpose of a Bump Contract is to force you to re-evaluate what you are doing in some area of your life by making things so challenging that you reach rock bottom and become willing to do things differently. When life gets uncomfortable enough, most people make decisions that help them learn the Soul Lessons related to their Lifetime Soul Contracts. For example, I dragged my feet for many years while I was deciding to leave the white-collar world to become a full-time intuitive. Finally, the day that my husband and I were purchasing our new, huge, expensive home, I was laid off from my job. For me, this was the ultimate Bump Contract. Yes, things were more difficult without a full-time job, but it felt like there was a reason everything happened on the same day. I took it as a push from my Soul to do the work I was born to do. It wasn't easy, but because of that bump, I knew it was right.

Heeding your Bump Contract is not mandatory. Your Soul views your bumps as your opportunities to align better with your Soul Lessons. There is no judgment if you didn't realize an experience in your life was actually a bump. Even though bumps may feel like terrible luck, their purpose is only to assist you—that is, if you can detach and find their message. If you miss the point, don't worry! Another opportunity will likely show up, but know the next bump may be bigger. At some point, they will make you uncomfortable enough to take action and get on track!

You may not always welcome the experience that the Bump Contract is trying to teach you, but the payoff is exponentially more than the work you put in. Bumps don't steer you wrong—and they save you from more trouble down the road. Based on this idea, all events small and big in your life have a greater purpose—to help you master a lesson. The Bump Contract ties into a greater Soul Lesson in some very deep way.

Lifetime Soul Contracts

Since this book focuses primarily on Lifetime Soul Contracts, when I mention *Soul Contracts*, I'm referring to the lifetime kind. For all other types, I will refer to them by their full names.

Lifetime Soul Contracts are the only form of contract that is not created before your Soul enters a new body. Instead, they are formed during a lifetime by repeated experiences and particular Seed Thoughts. For example, perhaps you have an embedded Seed Thought from when you were four years old. The Seed Thought makes you feel unsafe; as you grow older, you continue to suffer from it, always finding yourself feeling unsafe and unprotected. Finally, to counteract those experiences, you create a Lifetime Soul Contract.

You decide to to close yourself off from other people so you won't have to worry about feeling vulnerable.

When realized and mastered, Lifetime Soul Contracts help you learn a Soul Lesson and move forward from old, destructive patterns. These contracts can also teach you how to start working with your Relationship Soul Contracts. For example, once you've mastered your Lifetime Soul Contracts around your self-esteem, you can then take your new belief in your self-worth and apply it to your Relationship Soul Contract with your husband, who has been working to help you learn this as well. This is also why we are spending most of our focus in this book on Lifetime Soul Contracts—because they feed your work in Relationship Soul Contracts.

Your Lifetime Soul Contracts will manifest as challenges, blocks, or discomforts. Feeling challenged is the most common form of these contracts, since we tend to learn best when things are challenging. People who are completely happy and satisfied don't wake up in the morning and say, "Everything is so wonderful in my life. I'm going to change it!" Instead, we wait for our circumstances to become unbearable before we make changes. Soul Contracts have a way of making you feel like you have no choice but to make some dramatic changes in your perception and life choices.

EXERCISE: FINDING YOUR BLOCKS

Now that you know all about the various types of Soul Contracts, you can see that they manifest as blocks in your life and are usually much easier to pinpoint than Seed Thoughts, which occur when we have negative beliefs about ourselves that we then try to ignore. It's easiest to find your blocks by looking for the places where you feel stuck—maybe you're always overlooked for a promotion at your job. Contracts also show up in places where you repeat the same undesirable pattern, like dating women who are only interested in your money. Based on what you've learned so far, you should have a pretty good idea of what represents your major blocks.

It's now time to start defining your blocks. As you've been reading, you may have had an insight into your challenges: love, finances, opening your heart, success, and so on. For this exercise, we're going to put your insights to use. If you haven't had an ah-ha moment yet, you'll still be able to do the exercise! In fact, it may even inspire you.

Begin by listing your challenge areas. Look for patterns in your life that repeat. Do you have a terrible time accepting compliments? Do you make a lot of money, but spend it as soon as your paycheck clears? Are you exhausted because you drive yourself so hard to succeed? Write it all down, without judgment.

Some people have a lot of self-awareness. They can easily write their lists and don't have trouble seeing the patterns in their lives. But that's only a few people. Most people feel stuck instead. As you work, don't worry that you're going to miss a block or not get things perfectly right for your life. There are many different ways to complete this exercise.

First, examine your interactions with other people. Many people discover their negative repeating patterns by taking a look at their relationships! For example, are you having trouble with your boyfriend because he doesn't treat you right? Or do you hate your boss because she doesn't recognize the work that you do? Perhaps you have a friend who calls you at all hours to complain about her life, and you can't figure out how to avoid answering the phone? Write down all the people who give you stress.

Next, see if you can find the repeating pattern. Have most boyfriends treated you disrespectfully? Did former bosses—and perhaps even colleagues—overlook your skills in the past? To make this easier, you can make a list of each person you have had a stressful relationship with and what happened. Let's use Gerry as an example. She is having challenges around love, so she makes a bullet-pointed list of typical issues with her past relationships. Her list might look something like this:

- Went out with Larry. He appeared loving at first, but he was very attached to his job and didn't have time for me.
- Dated John for three years. He didn't communicate well. I had to draw him out to figure out what he was thinking.
- Saw Jorge for three months. He was talkative at first, but by the end, I felt like he was avoiding me.

Next, Gerry will want to find the common themes on her bullet-pointed list—in this case, a relationship pattern. All three men failed to give Gerry the time, love, attention, and support she wanted. Another thread is that Gerry kept choosing to stay, hoping that the relationship would change.

Use this exercise on two to three of your most challenging areas so that you can start to see how they manifest in your life. Don't worry about defining your blocks. The exercise is only intended to get you thinking about your negative, repeating patterns. As you work, you are developing an awareness of the areas of your life you will work on.

3

Getting the Lesson

Transforming your Soul System is not an overnight matter. You can't just say, "OK, Universe! I release everything blocking me!" and expect your challenges to magically fall away. Your job is to clear as much blocked energy as possible, understand what caused it, and master your Soul Lessons. When you have truly mastered the lesson, the block will be released. There is a difference between intellectually realizing that you follow an unhealthy pattern and must take XYZ steps to release it and then finally taking those steps. This is the difference between intellectual understanding and actual embodiment of the lesson. A great example of this is the difference between knowing that you *should* give up smoking and finally quitting.

Soul Contracts make things in a particular area of your life so uncomfortable that you change your behavior. When you finally throw your hands up, you have reached rock bottom, the emotional space where you feel that you have no other choice. Rock bottom looks different for everyone. One person may hit bottom when he is threatened with homelessness; someone else, when she gets a negative mark on her credit report. When an outcome becomes so undesirable that you will do anything—even the thing you've probably been resisting for months or years—to change the situation, you've hit your rock bottom. That means you are finally open to addressing and mastering the contracts related to this area of your life.

One of my clients, Christine, had an interesting experience with rock bottom. She discovered she had a Soul Contract that told her the only way to avoid getting hurt was to close herself off emotionally from all men. Throughout her entire life, her history with men consisted of being cheated on and lied to, which produced the Seed Thought, *I'm not safe*. As a result, she created a Soul Contract, closing herself off from love. By the time Christine was forty, her fear of being lied to had become the driving force in her relationship with any man—whether he was a colleague, family member, or potential boyfriend. She continued to meet seemingly wonderful men; however, she thought she couldn't trust any of them.

Just before Christine started working with me, she walked away (for the second time) from an engagement. Her reasoning was that she couldn't trust her fiancé because he worked such long hours. Although she was sad, she felt that breaking off the relationship was the only way to protect herself from being hurt. Her friends all disagreed with her choice. She lost several close girlfriends because they couldn't understand how she could throw away a man who was so clearly loving and devoted to her. By the time Christine and I began our work together, she had hit rock bottom. Friendless and loveless, she knew she had to make a change in order to experience trust in her relationships. To Christine, reaching rock bottom was a terrible time in her life, but it also represented the moment when she finally began work on her Soul System and started reconnecting to her brilliance.

If you ignore the opportunity to change what your rock bottom offers, the stress you're feeling will only escalate. If you still have the power to say, "not now," that moment is not your rock bottom. You'll experience more and more challenging opportunities until you are finally willing to make a massive change. Taking advantage of your rock-bottom moment isn't just about identifying the challenge at hand, realizing that you don't want things to go on this way, or feeling unhappy—those ideas are rungs on the ladder as you descend toward the bottom. It doesn't matter if you understand what is holding you back in life; until you are willing to take action, you have not reached the bottom, so those stopgap changes will not stick.

We know that we shouldn't keep picking a certain type of boyfriend, that a friend really isn't good for us, or that accepting a job just for the money won't actually bring abundance, but we make those choices anyway, hoping for different results than last time. The pattern can be broken when we reach rock bottom—until then, we have not driven ourselves down to a place where we will actually make a change.

Soul Contracts are not horrible, negative agreements we make to trip ourselves up. They are energies that help us master some lesson we struggle with. In one sense, they help us get to the top of the mountain faster. We still have to climb the mountain, but it's less steep, and we have ropes and shoes called Soul Contracts to help us. In Christine's case, her Soul Contract, which was supposed to protect her from a broken heart, served a greater purpose—to help her identify her underlying Seed Thought, *I'm not safe*. Through her work in her Soul System, she learned that she wanted to be open to real intimacy, and that she had a deep-seated belief that she couldn't trust men. By the time she mastered her Soul System, she shifted how she approached her relationships because she had transformed her beliefs about herself. Her rock bottom experience of losing the man she loved and three of her close friends made her realize that her only choice was to try something new.

EXERCISE: ROCK BOTTOM

As you're probably realizing, you've already had many rock bottom moments. Naming these moments can help you gain a greater understanding of yourself and could be key to your success in working with your Soul System. Take twenty minutes to write down any life moments where you reached bottom. Remember: If you did not make a complete change, you weren't at the bottom. If the situation helped you realize that you *should* make a change, but you didn't take action, that moment was not your bottom.

Your past successes can give you the courage, experience, and insight to challenge your current contracts. As you write your list, ask yourself: What happened? What event or experience pushed me to make a change?

Since we all have many seeds, contracts, and lessons, you'll probably be able to identify several moments in your past where you hit your rock bottom and seized the opportunity it presented.

If you're stuck, you may want to spend a few minutes writing down the experiences in your past when you thought you hit your rock bottom, but the changes you initiated did not last. Examining your experiences in this way will help you understand how you work and how often you fall into intellectual understanding versus embodiment. This exercise will give you a chance to examine your own past successes and build upon them.

Because there is a lesson to be learned from each and every contract, you can't break them all in one fell swoop. The lessons that we learn through our lives are what give us unique perspectives, wisdom, and expertise. If you erased the lesson prematurely, some of the immediate strife would be relieved, but it would not serve you in the long run. You'd miss out on rediscovering your brilliance, believing in your inner beauty, and feeling protected by the Universe. Furthermore, your challenge would eventually return in full force. This is why we release our blocks by working with both the obvious Soul Contract block and the underlying Seed Thoughts and Discordant Emotions. If you don't do it this way, you won't achieve release at the Soul level and your challenges will certainly remain.

In my private sessions, my clients often say things like, "Being single used to be an issue for me, but it's not anymore. I kind of like being alone" or "Sacrificing myself for others is something I used to do all the time, but I've stopped." They tell me that because of these new choices they're making, they are ready to release the Soul Contract. This isn't how the process works. It's not enough to just understand a problematic behavior, belief, thought, or pattern—you have to understand why it exists in the first place.

Think of it like a jar filled with water and sand. The hard layer of sediment at the bottom of the jar represents your contracts. After a time, it is difficult to distinguish the sand from the bottom of the jar. To break into that layer, you have to vigorously shake the jar. Once the particles are loose in the water, you can unscrew the top and filter out what you don't want. Observing, understanding, and taking action on the contracts in your life is like vigorously shaking the jar and filtering out that heavy sediment.

How do you release the contracts from your Soul? Can you say you're done with them and walk away? Do you just pour everything out and start from scratch? For most people, as soon as they understand what their hidden block is, they want to get rid of it immediately—as long as it doesn't cause too much pain. They try to change the habits created by the contract. But to truly master a contract and create the Soul-level change you're looking for, you'll have to alter certain aspects of your life, discover what is driving your contract, and make changes through sustainable steps. The result? Radical upgrades throughout your life.

My client Andrea was having difficulty finding love. She consistently chose men who were not a good match. She viewed every man she dated as a project. In her relationships, she took control and taught her boyfriends how to behave, get their lives together, and develop mature friendships. She even schooled them on their manners. Andrea was also very aggressive in her career—and very successful. She worked in a sales office with mostly men and had to be forceful and independent (to the point of being domineering) in order to succeed. She was proud of her strong, bossy nature and felt that it was one of her best qualities because it had created her career success.

When Andrea and I first spoke, it became evident that she didn't enjoy taking control in all her relationships; it just seemed like the best way to get the results she was looking for. Taking control was also a successful tactic in her work life. She wanted a man who would support her emotionally, physically, and mentally, but the men she chose were not capable of this. Her independence was one of her Soul Contracts blocking her.

When I told her this, she said defensivley, "We can release that in my love life, but I still need to be independent at work and in other areas." She could intellectually understand how taking control of her romantic relationships wasn't serving her, but she didn't see how it wasn't always benefiting her in the other parts of her life either. A Soul Contract permeates a person's entire life; however, it may only create stress or problems in one area. For example, many people in Andrea's office were intimidated by her. She found herself somewhat ostracized, but it also made it easy to get her work done quickly. Until Andrea realized that she was seeking balance—and grasped what her Soul Contract was really about—she was unable to get rid of the block she desperately wanted to clear.

To open herself to the love she wanted, Andrea had to address her independence issues. At first, her fear prevented her from doing this. She worried that she would have to behave differently at work, and that once the contract and underlying seeds were cleared, she would no longer be an independent, successful person.

Releasing contracts and seeds doesn't have to create a Jekyll-and-Hyde situation. When Andrea mastered her Soul System, she released this particular block. She didn't stop being able to take care of herself or being a good businesswoman, but her decisions were no longer driven by negative energy. She was still motivated at work, but allowed some of her coworkers to give her advice. She even asked a project manager to assist her on a particularly difficult project.

Being assertive and driven can be very good qualities—when they are balanced behaviors that come from a place of self-acceptance and inner peace. Andrea's behaviors were similar to how she'd acted before she worked with her Soul System, but her motivation changed. Rather than needing to control others in order to feel safe, she came to enjoy doing only some things herself.

Many people have been working on some iteration of their Root Belief System for several lifetimes. Soul Contracts, Discordant Emotions, Seed Thoughts, and even the Root Belief System can stay hidden from you until you are finally ready to deal with them. Many of my clients haven't realized whatever block they're dealing with stems from a decision they made early in life (or even in a past life). This work varies depending on the contract, the person or people involved, and the events surrounding it. Here are some examples of the success that people have experienced by working with their Soul Systems:

- A woman broke through her Miniwall Soul Contract (a contract to keep other people emotionally at bay) and released her Seed Thought of *I'm not good enough*, finally realizing that she had kept people—men in particular—out of her heart in order to protect herself. The result? She met a man who helped foster her newly budding belief in herself, and today they are happily married. A woman found unconditional love in her partner because she learned to love herself, something that many people struggle with today.

- A man finally got his business up and running, making over one million dollars a year because he released his *I'm not good enough* Seed Thought and his "failure" Soul Contracts.

- Upon the releasing of her *I'm not safe, supported, protected* Seed Thought and her "invisibility" Soul Contract, a woman began to write a book about her early childhood sexual abuse and found a publisher who wanted to work with her.

- Through the release of his Seed Thought, *I'm not a good person*, and his Soul Contracts of "give to everyone but myself and don't speak up," a man was able to start treating himself in a way that regained the respect and love of his estranged daughter.

There is no limit to what working with your Soul System will do for you. The more progress you make, the harder it will be to remember how difficult your situation was in the first place.

Changes, Changes, Changes!

We attract energies that are a vibrational match for the energy we hold within ourselves. Let's say you struggle with putting yourself first because your Root Belief System causes you to believe that you are a bad person if you take care of yourself before helping others. If you have this belief, you will automatically attract people who align with it. The people in your life will expect you to put them first and will rebel when you don't follow this model. After all, that's why they found you in the first place. Once you master one of your Root Belief Systems and learn to make decisions based on your greatest and highest good, the people who are only comfortable with your old vibration will begin to fall away.

It can be very difficult when everything around you seems to try to force you to go back to your old ways. Humans are creatures of comfort. We stick with what we know—even if it's not easy—because we are used to it. As you work on your Soul System, you will collide with many external forces that push you back into old behavior. If you're working on saying no, for example, you may find that your boss suddenly has twenty hours of extra work for you. Or perhaps a friend will suddenly decide she can't get through life without you at her side, 24/7. Even your partner may flat-out threaten to leave you if you don't start behaving like you used to.

There are real consequences to working on your Soul System, so it's a good idea to prepare yourself for what is coming. Other common side effects are changes in your primary relationship (meaning one of you leaves, or perhaps you both start working harder to improve what you have), quitting a job or getting a new one, releasing depression, discovering new friends, or breaking up with friends. In the long run, these changes will benefit you, even though they may feel difficult at first. Dealing with them is part of mastering your Soul Contracts, so get ready—to learn Soul Lessons, we can't bypass massive shifts in consciousness, environment, and happiness.

EXERCISE: MAKING CHANGES

Where do you want to start your work? Are you thinking love life? Career? Believing in yourself? Feeling safe? Trusting the outside world? Making more money?

In this exercise, start writing down the areas of your life that you think are going to change and any fears you have. For example, you might want to work on putting yourself first. One of your fears associated with doing things differently might be that you'll lose your job, that your friends will hate you, or that your mom will think you're selfish.

This exercise is not meant to make you feel scared, but to show you the reasons you haven't tried making a change yet. Listing your fears can put them in perspective. When you write in your journal, "I'm going to lose all my friends," part of you knows this doesn't have to be true. You can also see that losing old friends will open you up to new, wonderful, giving friendships.

The intention of this list is *not* to freak you out, but it has the potential to do that. Try to work through your fears and lay it all out. The reality of the change is nowhere near as difficult or scary as your list of imaginary fears.

4

Why Do We Have Lifetime
Soul Contracts?

As we've already discussed, Lifetime Soul Contracts (which we're calling Soul Contracts) are formed by you during a time (in either a current or a past lifetime) when you felt lonely, scared, depressed, trapped, or insecure or had any other negative emotion as a result of a Seed Thought. In a positive state of mind, you are the most connected to Source and your intuition and tend to make decisions that are helpful and good. Soul Contracts, however, are created when you react to a particular Seed Thought by making a little deal with yourself about what you can do that will counteract the pain or discomfort that you're feeling.

To break down this process, we'll start with the main energetic vibrations involved in it. When you were born, in order for your Soul to merge with your human body, your high, pre-birth vibrational state lowered to merge with the physical density of your human body and life on Earth. As your energetic body moved down the vibrational scale, you moved away from unconditional love, hope, and enlightenment and closer to the energies of grief, fear, and hate. Lower vibrations are further away from Source, which means that *just by being human*, you are less intuitively connected than you were pre-birth. In that lower vibration, you're more likely to experience certain emotions and energies. Lifetime Soul Contracts are created through having a human experience, and really can invoke a lot of havoc for a Soul made of pure Divine Light.

Creating a Lifetime Soul Contract

Imagine that you are going through a severe, difficult time in your life. At the same time, a Seed Thought that says *I'm not good enough* keeps showing up. You're fed up, upset, and frustrated. You feel badly about yourself, and every experience you have and person you meet seems to remind you that you aren't good enough. Your Seed Thought sends that negative message out to the Universe, and the Universe reflects it back to you.

This is when most people create a Lifetime Soul Contract. It's easy to understand why: you desperately want to stop the feeling that you aren't good enough. In a fit of anger, frustration, or despair, you devise a plan. Perhaps you say, "I'm going to be number one at my job, no matter what the cost" or maybe "I'm going to sacrifice my needs to support everyone else. That will prove how good I really am."

Because you aren't in a calm, clear, grounded, higher-vibrational state (you are, after all, experiencing very negative, low-vibrating emotions) and have decided to rely on your willpower, you create the contract. Many people don't realize what they are doing. They believe they are making these bargains in order to feel better, but in reality they are flagging an area of their life that they will have to revisit later.

To create a Lifetime Soul Contract, you must be in a significantly negative state, resulting from recurring experiences related to a particular Seed Thought. You wouldn't create a Soul Contract if you simply had a bad day at work. It takes a rock-bottom negative vibration, paired with feelings of desperation—as though the only choice you have is to make this agreement. Because of these special conditions, you probably don't have as many Soul Contracts as you think. It takes a lot of negative forces coming together to create one. This is to your benefit.

On the flip side, Lifetime Soul Contracts are hidden once we create them. Most people have no idea that they generated one in the first place. They just know that they desperately want things to change. They know that something isn't working. They see the same pattern over and over, but no matter what they do, they aren't able to stop it. Even though they feel powerless, they are determined to take control. The desire for relief results in a Lifetime Soul Contract, not because you initiated a change, but because you didn't understand the lesson behind the Seed Thought that was causing your pain.

When you slow down and start investigating the situation, you are taking the time to master the Seed Thought and release it. This raises your vibration, moving you closer to Source. Any decisions you make from that higher vibrational place and positive state of mind will not result in a Lifetime Soul Contract but forward movement in your life instead.

You have already formed Soul Contracts in this life. One good example is my client David. David's company was on the rise. He was a cutting-edge risk taker, and it was paying off. He had eight thousand employees, and he was making more money than he had ever dreamed of. Magazines featured articles about David's ability to predict the market. His parents lauded him. Women approached him because they sensed his prowess and confidence, his edginess. But suddenly, things shifted.

He made a strategic misstep, and he was forced to let go of more than half his employees. David was distraught and depressed. He felt guilty for causing pain to so many people. He thought, *If only I had slowed down or made more logical decisions—if only I had been grateful for what I had and didn't make all those deals, none of this would have happened.* He started to believe that he couldn't trust himself because he really didn't know what he was doing. This created a Seed Thought that said, *I'm not good enough.* He experienced failure after failure in his work because he stopped trusting his instincts. Finally, he decided, *I'm never going to make a mistake like that again. I'm never going to take risks like that. I have to be cautious!* And that was the creation of a Soul Contract.

His plan was to prevent causing pain to himself and others in the future—so he stopped taking risks. He decided that following the herd was the answer and shouldered a huge Lifetime Soul Contract.

As David's career progressed, he found that he couldn't recreate his former success by avoiding risk, not listening to his intuition, and following trends. When he did feel like taking a gamble, he hesitated. He completely eliminated the gut instinct that once helped him in business.

In the end, it took David's work with his Soul System to identify his Seed Thought of *I'm not good enough* and his Soul Contract that told him not to trust himself. They were stopping him from experiencing success in his life again. Once he learned that he was good enough, his trust in himself and good instincts returned. He was able to create success in his life again.

Most people don't realize what they are really doing when they make Soul Contract commitments. They are trying to take control at a time when they are not in a powerful position in their lives. Think about it: When you're upset or worried, are you smart? Can you act in your most capable manner? Do you make the same decisions you would if you were feeling calm, clear, and grounded? No. When you're in a negative emotional state, deciding what is best is incredibly difficult. The odds that you'll make the optimal decision are greatly reduced. Fear, sadness, anger, guilt—these block your ability to use logic and instinct, so you're left to base your actions on your fears.

Making this type of decision takes away your ability to change your mind in the future. When you create a Lifetime Soul Contract, you are unknowingly sealing this behavior, belief system, action, or thought into the deepest place possible—your Soul. Once you make the contract, your Soul is going to do everything possible to adhere to it, including undermining your conscious efforts to behave differently.

We can think of Lifetime Soul Contracts as energetic bookmarks. They stay buried within your Soul until you finally start addressing them. If you made a Soul Contract five lifetimes ago that you haven't addressed yet, that means you were born into this life with a Soul Contract block you don't know anything about. People often find blocks that aren't relevant to their current lifetime. Perhaps, as a toddler several lifetimes ago, you were severely scolded for talking too much. From this, you created a Lifetime Soul Contract to prove your goodness by not talking. Three lifetimes later, you're struggling with speaking up. That Lifetime Soul Contract is still hanging around, waiting for you to address it.

Countless contracts created in your other lifetimes remain intact in your Soul today. This is one of the reasons that people tend to be unaware of their blocks—they entered this lifetime with these challenges already in place. Many people have never actually experienced life free and clear of hurdles and hidden barriers.

Past-Life Soul Contracts can be a major contributor to your Root Belief Systems. If your Soul has been around for eighty-eight lifetimes, and you've struggled to believe in yourself during half of them, it's extremely likely that you're going to have at least one full-blown Root Belief System with contracts all contributing to that lesson. Luckily, there is a bright side to Past-Life Soul Contracts. Just because the contracts originated in another lifetime doesn't mean they are harder to discover, understand, and master. In fact, as you work through your Soul System, you will find that your Past-Life Soul Contracts are actually embedded within your Present-Life Soul Contracts. By working on the ones you've created in this lifetime, you're addressing those from the past as well.

EXERCISE: PAST OR PRESENT?

Knowing if one of your contracts is from a past life or present life can give you more detail and ease your mind. After all, it's pretty unlikely that you are going to have memories about past lifetimes. (Like being a knight and pledging to sacrifice yourself for the good of all other humans!) Writing down what you think the origins of your challenges are can often help you figure out your Soul System. Using the blocks you listed in the previous exercise, think about when you started suffering from them. Has a particular challenge been an issue for as long as you can remember? This might indicate the block is from a past life or stems from a pre-verbal time in your current life. Is there an obvious connection with a particular experience in your life? Or does the block make no sense because nothing in your past occurred to trigger it? When a challenge doesn't seem logical, it probably stems from a past life. For example, if you feel that you must be true to your word (no matter what you have to sacrifice), and you've never had anyone call you a liar or been cheated, it's very possible that your block originated in a past life.

Also, remember that many of your Past-Life Soul Contracts end up getting entangled in your Present-Life Soul Contracts—so if you only come up with contracts that make sense in this lifetime, that's just fine. It doesn't mean you don't have any contracts from your past lives. The blocks you have are just linked with the ones in this lifetime. You'll address them as you address your present blocks.

You will have amazing results no matter which lifetime you start working on. Determining which lifetime your block originated in isn't critical, but it can certainly help you feel like you have a handle on your Soul System. As you move forward, try to figure this out; it could give you a greater understanding of your current situation. So, as a kick-start, spend five to ten minutes thinking about the origin of your contracts.

5

Step 1: Set Your Foundation

Understanding & Acceptance

Working on your Soul System requires understanding and acceptance. As you begin, remember that we *all* have Soul Contracts. These blocks often remain hidden for decades—so perhaps you aren't as much of a screw-up as you thought. Other energies at work have prevented you from succeeding. They may have pushed you to make certain bad decisions over and over again. Your Soul is perfect, wherever you are in this process. If it doesn't seem that way right now, it's because you have done things that hide that perfection from yourself.

It's time to stop beating yourself up. Stop worrying that you're never going to get it or that you weren't meant to achieve your goals. Stop feeling guilty about your past decisions. To transform your Soul System, you have to be able to turn over the responsibility, in some way, to your Soul. Accept that something is happening on a deeper level in your Soul. For example, spending your time thinking about how frustrated you feel when you keep getting into the same fights with your mother doesn't address your Soul System issues. However, saying, "I think there is a Soul Contract at work here. I'm going to look into it!" shows progressive understanding. Once you have acknowledged that greater forces are at work—and that you are only human and allowed to make mistakes—you can start moving forward. This is all a plan to help you evolve. You're shifting your energy, making it pliable so you can do this work. When you experience acceptance, you're ready to start working.

To work at the deepest, most effective levels, you need to upgrade your Guide Team and clear your fields. Skipping these steps means you'll be addressing your day-to-day habits rather than your Soul Systems. Think of it as treating the symptoms without curing the disease. Many people realize they have certain blocks and try to force themselves to make behavior changes to resolve them. However, this can create problems if the underlying energies are not addressed.

Simply behaving differently, rather than shifting the driving factors below, only results in superficial changes. What we want instead is a deep, Soul-level shift that allows you to grow. Let's start by addressing the causes of these blocks and initiate real change from the inside out.

Upgrading Your Foundation

The first step in setting a strong foundation for Soul System work is ensuring that the energies you work with have the highest vibration and purest intention. We attract energies to us that are similar to what we put out; that principle extends into the world of Spiritual Guides as well. Your Spiritual Guides are beings made of light, who have never had a physical body before. Each person has many Spiritual Guides that play different roles in their lives. One Guide may be your main Guide, assisting you with everyday tasks. Another Guide may help you write a book, be an incredible mother, or survive abuse. When they're part of your Guide Team, Spiritual Guides will always look out for your greatest and highest good and give you the very best information when you ask for it.

Many of us, however, have a few Guides who slipped into our Guide Team. They are not officially part of it. They come when we are challenged, angry, upset, or hurt. Have you ever yelled out to the world, "Ugh! I just want some help! Won't anyone help me?" You may have sent out this message in a conscious or unconscious state. Even if you didn't speak the words, you energetically voiced your need. When you did this, you unknowingly attracted energies that matched your negative state. In your lower energy state, you took in energies of lower vibrations because they felt good at the time—but remember, the lower the vibration, the less pure light it holds. These lower vibrating energies naturally contributed to lowering your overall vibration.

For your Guide Team, you want Guides who are of the highest vibration, possessing 100 percent Divine Light. When you attract energies that are not of 100 percent Divine Light, you disadvantage yourself. You're trusting impure energies to guide you and give you access to the deepest level of the Soul. It's a recipe for making more blocks, impeding forward movement, and creating a whole lot of frustration.

What if you have a negative energy guiding you? Luckily, it's easier to get rid of these tagalongs than most people believe. You'll have great results. All it takes is diligence and commitment to this simple task: upgrading your Guide Team.

The Light Calls

A decade ago, I was introduced to the idea of upgrading my Guide Team at a workshop. It was an advanced clearing technique, included in our coursework as an optional lesson. Most people in the class skipped over it, but it resonated deeply with me. I found myself expanding the technique and eventually applied it to my work with many of my clients. Later, I read Lynn Grabhorn's book *Dear God! What's Happening to Us?*, which includes specific affirmations to help people reset their Guide Teams.[1] Initially, I had my clients work with Grabhorn's invocations, but over the years, I've been guided to create the Light Calls. (I named them the Light Calls because that is simply what you are doing with them—calling in the Light.) This technique can shift the energies for work within the Soul System. The Light Calls are one of the easiest, most effective ways to create a strong foundation for Soul System work.

The results of upgrading your energy in this way can be awesome. Although many people have studied spiritual principles and energy techniques, they may not have met much success. This is because they do not realize that their Guide Teams are full of Light. I wrote the Six Calls for you to use to align yourself with the highest vibrations. Before you begin the technique, please read each Call and how to use it.

---

1. Lyn Grabhorn, *Dear God! What's Happening to Us?: Halting Eons of Manipulation* (Newburyport, MA: Hampton Roads Publishing, 2003).

How to Use the Six Calls

Basically, the Calls summon only beings, events, experiences, and Guides of the purest, highest vibration. Once you have reoriented your Divine Light and the Light around you, you'll find that working with your Soul System is much easier. You can trust your intuition. You'll have more meaningful experiences with clearer meanings. Best of all, you'll be working with a Guide Team that is sure to look out for your greatest and highest good.

Intuitively and through my years of experience working with the Light Calls, I have found that most people have the greatest success by doing the Calls daily for forty days. Some people prefer to choose a number of days using their intuition. Either method will work. When you reach the final day, evaluate your progress. Do you feel like you experienced enough change? Are you feeling good? You can always keep going with this technique. Use your gut to determine how many more days to continue.

The Calls are most effective when spoken out loud. Like all the tools and processes in this book, the vibration of the words adds to the exercise's effectiveness. And the Calls take only a couple minutes to complete. Where you are when you say them is not important; you can even lock yourself in the bathroom if privacy is an issue!

It's also really important that you stay consistent with the Calls. Each day's energy builds on the energy before it. A missed day will interrupt the flow as it shifts and develops. If you miss a day, start over again at day one. You can't fool the energy into thinking that you're committed to the change. If you're not taking the steps seriously, the transformation won't happen!

As you are going through the process of performing these Light Calls, you're going to find that things in your life do shift—

sometimes they even shift dramatically. You may experience a bit of chaos and unrest at first, but as you continue with this work, those experiences will subside.

EXERCISE: THE SIX CALLS

Begin by calling on your Guide Team. If you know how to do this already, go for it. If you are unsure how to do this, you can simply say, "I am now calling on my Guide Team that aligns with 100 percent Divine Light to assist me with this work today." Use your imagination to see, hear, or feel your team as they surround you to help you call the Light.

State the following Six Light Calls out loud:

1. By the Power of Grace, I consciously state that my entire being at all levels shall be reset to wholly align with 100 percent Divine Light, *now*.
2. By the Power of Grace, I consciously state that my consciousness and unconsciousness, highest self, and physical and energy bodies shall be reset to wholly align with 100 percent Divine Light, *now*.
3. By the Power of Grace, I consciously state that my Guide Team shall be made up of only beings that wholly align with 100 percent Divine Light, *now*.
4. By the Power of Grace, I consciously state that any spiritual attachments I have created that do not align wholly with 100 percent Divine Light be released, for the greatest and highest good of all, *now*.
5. By the Power of Grace, I consciously state that my environment through infinity shall be reset to wholly align with 100 percent Divine Light, *now*.
6. By the Power of Grace, I consciously state that only beings, energies, and experiences that wholly align with 100 percent Divine Light may be allowed within my fields, *now*.

Light Call Results

Many people resist trusting their intuition. They struggle with trusting that the Universe will bring them the experiences that match what they're asking for. They even have trouble believing in themselves. As your Guide Team is strengthened and reconnected to you, you'll find that it's easier to receive intuitive information. Additionally, that information will be more accurate, since you will be receiving it from only beings of the highest vibration. As you revamp your own energy field, you'll also find that you can trust your gut more often. You will attract less chaos, and many things in your life may start to click. This is because you're free of those negative energetic influences. When you, your Guides, and the energy around you are adjusted to vibrate at a higher level, what you are seeking in your life will shift more easily as well.

Watch out for the reprogramming process, though. While the results are positive and life changing, the transition can be a little hairy. You may find that things that have worked for you for years suddenly fall away, and that can be very scary. The first time that I went through the Six Calls, the number of people signing up for private sessions with me dropped dramatically. I was floored by this change. As it turned out, the reason the clients had shifted was because I had unknowingly pulled in some lower-vibrating energies. Those low-vibrating energies helped me attract low-vibrating clients who didn't feel wonderful for me to work with and served to increase my anxiety around my business. A few weeks after I completed the Light Calls, however, I had an influx of new, higher vibrating clients who resonated with me better. This is what I had wanted in the first place, without even realizing it. Sometimes it may seem like the Calls are causing you to lose something or someone you valued, but continue your work without fear. Whatever you lost will be replaced by something much better that matches your vibration.

Also, you don't need to complete your forty days (or whatever number of days you intuitively chose) of Calls before you can work on your Soul System, but the Six Calls are an essential part of this work. The more light you hold, of course, the easier you'll transition to mastering your contracts. The Light Calls will work hand in hand with you as you work on the various steps of the system. Once you've committed to the Call process, you're ready to move on to your energetic foundation—the next step.

Your Energy Field

Now that you are working with 100 percent Divine, positive energies, you are ready to reset your foundation. When a person's energy field is clear, they feel emotionally and physically lighter. They also experience more happiness and hope, and they have easier access to their emotions. This, in turn, provides a strong energetic foundation. With one of these, you can make better decisions—and you'll need it if you plan to work at the Soul level. Think of this process as opening a path to the heart of your problems. If you don't have a clear road, you're never going to be able to make it to the core issues.

Clarity of mind, body, and spirit is an ideal state for Soul System work. This means we have to address your physical body as well as the state of your energy field. The energy around your body is made up of several different layers: energetic, physical, mental, emotional, and spiritual. This field fills the space three to four feet above, below, and around your body. It's an incredibly sensitive system that influences your thoughts, feelings, emotions, decisions, and behavior without your knowledge. The energies that occupy our energy fields are closest to us and most comfortable. We rely on them, so they become easy to reach for. Think of it this way—if you were holding an armful of red balls and someone asked you to think of a certain color, you would probably think of red. Or you might think, *Not red, anything but red!* Either way, you thought red first. The energies in your fields function the same way. They subconsciously guide you toward certain thoughts, behaviors, and habits.

What kinds of energy occupy your energy fields? They are superficial energies that you have absorbed and attracted. Your environment is made up of the people, situations, events, and feelings of everything around you, but nothing that is actually part of you. Many people are more sensitive than they realize, and they unknowingly absorb the negative emotions and energy of those around them.

Luckily, since these environmental energies aren't deep, they are much easier to clear and balance than contracts and Seed Thoughts—but that doesn't mean you should take them lightly. Negative energies in your fields can influence every thought, decision, and feeling. This can lead you to believe things in your life are much worse or more difficult than they really are. This is why you must balance your energies and release those that no longer serve you before you can work at the level of the Soul.

The energies that get stuck in your fields can be one or many of the following:

Discordant Energies: This is the most common type of energy that people unknowingly draw to their fields. Have you ever seen two people fighting and yelling at each other and found yourself feeling angry or distressed, even if you walked away? This is because you absorbed the fight's negative energy. Have you ever spent an hour on the phone listening to your depressed friend talk about her bad luck only to find that when you hang up the phone, you feel depressed as well? Most people are surprised to find how many Discordant Energies they are carrying with them. Worry, anxiety, stress, depression, and fear are the most common, but most people attract other types as well.

Belief Systems: Beliefs hold a particular energy vibration or frequency. Beliefs that are attached to low-frequency ideas (such as revenge) can be absorbed into your energy field. The belief system then causes you to continually refer back to that lower vibration. You can pick them up from other people, experiences, and even books or TV.

Negative Energies: Negative energies can be picked up from a location, an experience, or even a TV show. Several years ago, I used to fall asleep watching a crime investigation show and wondered why I always felt so low when I woke up. The negativity holds a low frequency and continually works to bring your own frequency into alignment with it. If you have this type of negative energy within your fields, you are actively drawn toward negative thoughts. As with other energy types, that negative energy will attract more of its own kind into your life and way of thinking.

Interference or Static Energy: Interference energy is energy that creates static in your experience. It clutters your thinking, your sense of clarity, and especially your intuition. A friend of mine recently told me that she had to move out of her new apartment because of the cell towers next to her building. Soon after moving in, she felt unclear, tired, and angry. Finally, she realized she was absorbing the interference energy of the towers into her fields. Interference energy is often absorbed by people who live near an airport or who have planes flying overhead. This phenomenon is often overlooked; as an adaptive species, we tend to get used to this type of interference and ignore it. On an energetic level, interference is energy that is impossible to ignore.

Electromagnetic Fields (EMFs): EMFs are generated by electronics such as cell phones and laptops. EMFs create static in our energy fields that can cause difficulty sleeping, fuzzy thinking, moodiness, and more. It is possible to clear your fields of the energy from EMFs, but continual exposure can have negative long-term effects. To deal with EMFs, you should move electronic objects at least eight feet from you while you sleep and try to refrain from using electronics whenever possible. I realize this is a difficult task—one that I can't completely follow myself, since I love my iPhone!—but it is the best way to reduce the EMFs that end up in your energy fields.

Programming: This energy can be very sneaky. Most people attract it during their childhoods, when they are young and easily influenced by others. I see a lot of people struggling with the programming of *no pain, no gain*. If you picked this one up during your childhood, you probably have a job where you are expected to put in seventy to eighty hours per week. Sound familiar? Many people will take the programming energy in their fields and create a Soul Contract around it as well.

There are many kinds—more than I've listed here. Hopefully, this basic information will help you identify and clear whatever energies you encounter. What's most important is being aware of your fields and doing what you can to clear them.

Energy Field Susceptibility

Why do some people absorb every environmental energy, while others do not? It's all about being empathic. An empath is a person who is capable of feeling the emotions of others despite the fact that they themselves are not going through the same situation. If you have ever walked into a room and felt like it was creepy in there, or disliked someone you just met, before they even opened their mouth, you have empathic abilities.

Imagine that you are talking on the phone with a friend who is going through a hard divorce. She complains, tells you about how mean her husband is, and cries about the effect the split will have on her children. Meanwhile, you're supporting your friend by listening. You feel compassion and you want to help. You feel angry at her husband for treating her unfairly. You worry about her children with her. By the end of the conversation, you feel like you really understood and helped her—or at least gave her a shoulder to cry on. You hang up the phone and think, *Phew! I am so tired!* This is a perfect example of being empathic—you just spent an hour absorbing your friend's negative energies into your fields.

Now here's the crazy part. She was feeling sad, lonely, angry, and victimized by her husband. As you listened to her, you slowly took in some of her energies. This allowed your friend to feel better, and you felt good because you were helping her. However, now that it's over, you're walking around your house, going to work, and driving in your car with a field full of Discordant Energies.

When energy enters your fields, it can feel like it's your own energy or emotion. For example, after the phone conversation with your friend, you were probably feeling sad and angry, and you may have even lashed out at your own family because of those feelings.

The problem is that those feelings aren't yours. They only seem like yours. As I said before, people tend to reach for their most readily available energy. If you are carrying your friend's sadness and despair around in your fields, your reactions to your own life will mimic those exact emotions.

Most people don't realize that they are allowing others' emotions and energies into their fields. In fact, our society has taught us that the best, most giving, and nurturing people function this way (hopefully, you are rethinking this myth).

EXERCISE: ARE MY FIELDS UNCLEAR?

How do you know if your fields are unclear? Well, if you have never done this work before, your fields probably need some cleanup. In our culture, we're expected to absorb other people's energies in order to help them. So, most people start out with unclear fields when beginning to declutter their Soul System. Here are some sure signs that can clue you in on the state of your energy fields:

1. Do you wake up in the middle of the night worrying about anything other than yourself? Worried about world peace? Worried about the state of the economy? Anxiety that focuses on ideas, people, and places beyond your control means you have attracted some external energies.
2. Do you get distracted easily? For example, if you are working on writing your book and it starts to snow, do the snowflakes falling outside your window completely take you away from the writing? If you are working on a detailed project, do you keep losing your train of thought? There are many distraction energies that we easily attract into our fields.
3. Do you feel disconnected from your body? Do you spend more time in your head, rarely thinking about your body? When you get dressed each morning, do you consider how you will look? These are signs

that you have taken in energies that distract you from focusing on yourself.

4. Does one particular emotion act like a filter for everything you experience? For example, does new information have to filter through your anxiety before you can process it? This pattern could mean that you have adopted the anxiety of someone or something outside yourself (such as a TV show).

5. Do you feel like there is always chaos around you? Many people with unclear fields can sense the lack of clarity, even if they can't put their finger on what's wrong. If your fields are not clear, nothing is ever organized, the world around you feels slightly out of control, and things just don't work properly. Of course, Soul Contracts can influence this chaotic feeling, but start by clearing your fields before you decide what its origin is.

If you even *think* your fields aren't clear, chances are they aren't.

Clearing your fields is not a one-time deal. Influential energies will always enter your fields, so clearing them is something that you should do as ongoing maintenance. I clear mine often—and when I find that my fields are severely unclear, I don't beat myself up. I just feel grateful that I realized what was going on, clear my fields, and move on. The more experience you have with this, the sooner you'll realize you have foreign energies hanging around, which means it will be easier to get rid of them. Being human does not mean behaving perfectly!

EXERCISE: FIELD CLEARING TECHNIQUE

This is an exercise that involves your energy, intention, and the Universe. You are going to clear your fields using a clearing request to state your intention to the Universe about what you want to happen. The clearing request only works if you clearly state your intentions and call on universal help. It also helps to have privacy.

1. Find a safe, private place where you will not be disturbed for about fifteen minutes. You want a space where you can be as crazy as you want and say the oddest and weirdest things, and no one will hear you or bother you. You should also turn off your cell phone and your email. I know when my iPhone goes off, my mind immediately wonders, *Oooh! Who's talking to me?* So it's best to just remove the temptation.

2. My suggestion is that you have complete quiet. Music holds the vibration of the notes, as well as the vibration and intentions of the people who composed and performed the music. We don't need to add any additional frequencies to your field. We want clarity.

3. Call on the Universe. You can say something simple, such as, "I am now calling on my Guides of 100 percent Divine Light to assist me with this work today." Your imagination is one of the best ways to work with energy because it frees you from inhibitions, so after calling on the Universe, take a moment to imagine the Universe responding to your request and what that feels like. Imagine it the way a little kid would— without judgment and with a whole lot of detail.

4. Say your field clearing out loud. The words that you will say carry a vibration that corresponds to your prayer. Stating your request out loud will make it more powerful than if you just said it in your head.

Next, I'll share a field-clearing appeal I use in my practice. Understand that these words are not written in stone. As you become familiar with this kind of communication, I encourage you to shift words and phrases around according to what feels right for you. This is a template for you; three years from now, you probably won't be saying the exact same clearing request. Honor your intuition; if a particular piece of this appeal bothers you, give that credit. Perhaps you need to rework something within your request. At the beginning, it's best to use the clearing request as I have written it, until you have become more familiar with what you're doing.

You're now ready to work with the field-clearing appeal.

Here is the clearing request to read aloud:

Please perform a whole and complete release at all levels for any
and all negativity that is interfering with me in any way, now.
Block all negative energy connections to me and completely
and fully release from my being all resulting spiritual and emotional attachments I have made as a result. Please dissolve the
negative energy into the Light, to be sent home, for the greatest
and highest good of all, now. Thank you, thank you, thank you.

Once you have read the request aloud, sit for a minute or two. Give
yourself time to experience what this moment is offering to you and
releasing from you. Your immediate results, if any, will be subtle. This
exercise will not give you a knock-you-over transformation—you're
seeking a subtle change. Many people who perform the clearing request
aren't attuned to their energy field and don't notice the shifts in it. If you
do not feel anything, it only means you don't know what signs to look for
or how to read them yet—it does not mean that the request didn't work.
Over time, you'll get better at detecting that your clearing request worked.
Here is a list of some typical changes that people experience as they release
interfering energies from their fields:

- Dizziness
- Lightheadedness
- Tingling in hands or anywhere in body
- Stillness
- A feeling of ease
- Less pressure on shoulders
- Less pressure on chest

- Less pressure on abdomen
- Seeming like the sun just came out—brighter in the room
- A feeling of wanting to cry
- A feeling of hope
- A feeling of serenity or less chaos
- Stillness in the air around your body
- Quiet
- Peace
- Tiredness
- Excitement
- Easier breathing

Some of these experiences may feel negative or uncomfortable (like dizziness), but that should not deter you from clearing your fields in order to set a strong foundation. The side effects of clearing your fields will only last about a minute. If you are very sensitive, you might feel them for up to five minutes.

For most people, it takes about five to ten minutes for the full effects of the field clearing to emerge. You'll facilitate a better release in that time period if you stay quiet, focus on yourself, and don't check your email or talk on the phone. This is your moment. You are reclaiming what is yours. These are your energies, emotions, and energy fields, and no other energies have a right to hitch a ride.

Check in with yourself a few minutes after making the request. Do you feel a little better, or do you feel the same way you did before?

If you still feel cluttered, stressed, and chaotic after you have done the field-clearing appeal, then it is possible that you didn't actually clear your fields. I meet a lot of people who do this exercise often, but say they don't feel different afterward. They say to me, "Danielle, every morning when I wake up, I clear my fields like you showed me. And I do it before bed, too. I'm doing everything you taught me, and I'm still struggling!"

I've found that people who say this to me are usually rule followers. They believe that if they do everything they are told, the way it's prescribed, everything will take care of itself. The problem is, we have to actually pay attention while we do this work, not just go through the motions. If Jane does her field-clearing appeal in the morning as she's dashing out the door to work, she's not taking the time and focus necessary to create the shift in her energy. Field clearing is not about just getting it done. If you do it and it doesn't actually create a shift in your emotions or energy, then you didn't give sufficient focus to the request or yourself.

In my practice and during my lectures, I've met plenty of people who go through the motions. Often, they've studied spiritual principles for years, read every book, visited every self-help guru out there, and built a routine of twenty different things that they do each day to help themselves feel better. Most of these people are not stopping to ask, "Does this work for me?" or "Did this exercise benefit me today?" Instead, they follow the dictates of the many different teachers, books, and classes in their life who have said, "*This* is the path to healing! Do *this* every day!" They overlook the cues from their own energy and emotions, which are saying, "Hey, slow down, buddy. You're not giving yourself a fighting chance at releasing this stuff."

If you tried the field-clearing request and it didn't work for you, look at your concentration. Were you giving the exercise 100 percent of your attention, or were you a little distracted? Did you create enough time in your schedule to feel calm about giving fifteen minutes to the field clearing? You can't half-ass field clearing. If you do, you might as well not have tried it at all. Your energy is smart—it knows when you mean something and when you're just going through the motions. So, if it didn't work, stop and try again, this time with your full attention.

EXERCISE: BLUE BUBBLE OF LIGHT

Now, let's talk about an energetic exercise that can help you stop absorbing (or absorb less of) the energies of others. This will help you maintain all the work you've done in previous exercises. It's all part of setting up a strong foundation for our Soul Contract work—and it means it's time to get into five-year-old-kid mode.

For this exercise, think back to when you were a child. At this time, you were more open to new things. Little-kid mode is the state of mind where you don't care what other people think, you do not censor yourself, and you're pretty much willing to try anything—if it's fun. If you are able to stay in that uncensored, just-go-with-the-flow mode, you'll really be able to benefit from this exercise.

Think of a purple dog. Now, think of a tricycle with a yellow seat. Think of a lime-green cat. See? All this exercise asks you to do is use your imagination. If you get stuck, you are trying too hard. Go do a cartwheel. Jump up and down in your office. Do something to remind yourself that this is fun! Then come back and start the exercise again. Do whatever it takes. And stop taking it all so seriously!

The intention of this exercise is to provide you with a loving, energetic barrier that resists the energies around you. The goal is not to shut out your environment; rather, it is to provide a filter so that you can more fully experience what is going on around you. Think of this exercise like sunglasses—they protect your eyes, but still allow you to see.

1. Start by ensuring that you are calm. Perhaps you need to be alone in the bathroom (usually a calm place) or in your car. Some of my clients don't have private space in their homes, so they've done things like climb into their closets and shut the doors, or they've gone for a walk outside alone. Being in a calm space is important; you will spend a few minutes

there, so make sure it's a comfortable zone. Don't move on to the next step until you have found a calm space and feel ready and relaxed.

2. At this point, many people like to call on their Spiritual Guides for assistance. If you aren't inclined that way, just sit and feel calm. If you are someone who enjoys working with Guides, angels, or spirits, imagine that they are with you now, ready to assist you as you make your appeal. If you're unsure how to do this, simply say, "I am now calling on my Guides of 100 percent Divine Light to assist me with this work today."

3. Now, envision a beautiful, blue bubble of light, about six feet tall and three feet wide, hovering across from you. Imagine that there is a peaceful feeling coming from this large bubble. It feels safe to look at and touch. Take twenty seconds or so to do this.

4. Visualize the blue bubble of light moving toward you. It gets closer and finally surrounds you. If you work with Guides, ask them to assist you in adjusting the bubble for a perfect fit.

5. Sit for a moment. Imagination is energy, just like everything else in our world. This bubble is energetically real and can have a real effect on you, your body, your emotions, and even your mental functions. Take notice of the safe, calm feeling you have being inside this bubble. The only energy that can easily pass through this bubble is love. That love can pass both ways—to you and from you. The inside of this bubble will feel very positive.

6. Once you've noticed the effect the bubble has on you, you are good to go. If you didn't feel anything, perhaps you were distracted while performing the exercise. Wait until you are focused and try again.

This exercise helps you create a loving barrier against the energies that are present at any given time in your environment. Whether those energies are coming from a friend, a TV show, a sad book, or your awareness of difficulty somewhere else in the world, the blue bubble will help you resist attracting them. The blue bubble will stay active around you for a couple of hours, so feel free to go about your life without thinking about it. By about two hours after you have invoked it, the bubble's barrier will have degraded, and it will no longer do a good job.

When you first experience a world where you're not picking up every single energetic signal, you may want to wear the blue bubble all the time. But that's not what it is for. The blue bubble will help you in situations where you know you usually attract other energies into your fields. Most commonly, that energy comes from certain friends or family, but it could also be when you go to the grocery store or a hockey game. I advise my clients to use the blue bubble whenever they are going to be around groups of people or in stressful situations; many of us absorb energies more easily when we are emotionally activated.

As you can see, it is important to set a strong foundation. Now you have several important (but fun!) tools to help you do that. When you incorporate the physical, energetic, and spiritual aspects of yourself into your foundation, it's easier to work within your Soul System and also to maneuver through your life in general. So many people accept their lack of clarity or chaotic energy as a normal part of life, but there is no reason to do that—especially when it's so easy to feel strong, clear, and grounded.

6

Step 2: Awareness I

Now that you have set your foundation, it's time to get a feel for what's going on in your Soul System. The first awareness step is akin to the way a carpenter will take a look at the floor plan, woodwork, and condition of his tools before he starts a new project. Without this knowledge, the carpenter wouldn't even know where to begin. It's the same for you. Where in your life are your blocks making the biggest ruckus? What is tripping you up most right now? Which areas of your life will you address first? What are your Seed Thoughts? Through awareness, you'll be able to identify all these things.

Your success during the awareness step is primarily based on your commitment to the process; however, there are other factors as well. During this step, you will begin to look at your life from a different perspective. As you do this, you'll realize things about yourself that you had no idea of before. In fact, most people have exciting ah-ha moments when they finally grasp that their block has deeper roots than they originally thought or when they realize that the blocks are not actually about what they assumed. How you embrace these new ideas will also affect your success. Obviously, resisting them will slow you down, while welcoming them will speed up your process.

Your epiphanies during the awareness step are incredibly helpful. Each one serves not just to inform you, but also begins to loosen the contracts within that particular Root Belief System. Loosened energy in a problematic area is exactly what you are looking for.

To effectively work the awareness step, you will need a general idea of the areas in which you are blocked. This isn't difficult—you probably picked up this book with some of your blocks in mind. You also started to make a list of your blocks in chapter 1. It's possible that you'll learn that your blocks are different—but for now, just go with what you know. You'll also need to identify the components of your Root Belief System (or maybe you can already see the entire thing!). You will learn how to do that in this chapter. You'll also learn how to expose the Seed Thoughts and Discordant Emotions anchoring your Soul Contracts to you.

The awareness step can be very quick. It may take you only five minutes to figure out your Root Belief System, blocks, and underlying Seed Thoughts—or it may take longer. It varies for each person.

How deeply are you willing to work? How complicated is your Root Belief System? Do you resist exposing it? The pace is up to you. You influence it consciously, unconsciously, and at the Soul level. Rather than being frustrated, know that your Soul is helping you have realizations and make changes at the appropriate pace. Move too fast and you'll only experience superficial changes.

I recently hosted a Soul Contracts Day on Facebook and invited people to ask me general questions about Soul Contracts. The purpose of the event was twofold. First, I wanted to offer people a safe place to ask their craziest questions about Lifetime Soul Contracts—especially since so many people get them confused with Relationship Soul Contracts. I also wanted to know what the most popular questions about Soul Contracts were. The one people asked the most was: How do I know what my Soul Contract is?

Four Ways to Identify Your Soul Contracts

There are four methods to figure out your Lifetime Soul Contracts. You may find that you have more than one contract; that is normal. As you identify them, it will be clear which one is most important and needs to be worked on first. You'll probably begin by figuring out the primary Soul Contract that is holding you back, but be open to the idea that you most likely have many more. Working on one contract opens the door to the others.

Method 1: You Might Already Know

This is the easiest way to identify your Soul Contracts. In fact, you probably picked up this book because you were feeling blocked in a particular area. Remember, if you are thinking you're blocked, you probably are.

Think back to what made you pick up this book. Were you feeling frustrated about your marriage? Were you worried you weren't getting anywhere in your life? Were you concerned that you were going to continue to pick the same icky man over and over? Something must have been going on in your head to attract you to this book—a book written to help you find hidden blocks in your life. Think back to that initial motivation. That *something* is where you'll start finding your Soul Contracts.

Let's consider my client Annika. She came to me because she was sad, really struggling to see the goodness she had to offer. She told me that she thought she was blocked because she couldn't be happy. She couldn't remember a time when she was happy and knew that she was blocked from experiencing a truly happy life. (I love when a client says this because it shows that they've already begun their work!) After helping Annika set her foundation, we got to work on those Soul Contracts she had been circling. I asked her to point out the places where she thought she was blocked. She said it wasn't just one place—it was *all* places. She wasn't happy in her work because she wanted more creative freedom. She wasn't happy in her marriage because her husband put her down, criticized her, and didn't treat her with respect. She recounted many instances where she felt unhappy.

When I asked her to talk about her past, she described a child-hood that lacked proper care (both physically and emotionally), where she was ignored by her parents. As we talked about her first memories, Annika connected the feelings she had when she was three years old to the emotions that she felt now: sadness, disappointment in the world, and abandonment. In the memory, her mother told her that the family was moving to South America—and then left without her.

Annika remembered making the determination at that young age that she wasn't good enough, so her mother hadn't taken her to Chile with her. At three, she felt abandoned by her mother and disappointed that her needs weren't being met. She thought she didn't merit her mother's or God's attention because she just wasn't good enough. In our session, Annika realized that her three-year-old self had decided it was impossible to be happy. She'd held onto a massive feeling of sadness connected with the lack of control she had in her life as a child. Annika identified a major component of her Root Belief System—her Soul Contract that said, "To avoid disappointment, hurt, and pain, I must never be happy."

Most people have a good sense of where their blocks are. It only takes a little intuitive logic and a basic understanding of the Soul System to figure out what is really going on. You know if you're stuck, obsessed, overly worried, or making decisions that aren't serving you. You know where you are blocked. Take some time to sort through that—does it permeate in other areas or only in one? Most people find that their blocks affect their entire life, even though they are just focusing on one area. We'll talk more about that later.

Method 2: Repeated Patterns

Another method for becoming aware of the components of your Root Belief System is to look at repeated patterns. Soul Contracts nudge us to behave in certain ways—usually not the healthiest ones. Even when we don't want to make certain choices, we do anyway. For example, many people keep choosing the same unhealthy love relationship. Some people keep finding new jobs because their employers are always taking advantage of them—but end up putting themselves back in the same position. I've seen people who've started five or six business only to have each one fail. Think of a repeated negative pattern as an arrow pointing to a contract.

My client Beatrice was like that. She kept choosing friendships that made her tired and resentful. Her best friend called her at all hours to ask for advice, her mother dropped her dog off for a week at Beatrice's house without asking, and her coworkers used her network to help themselves professionally but gave her nothing in return. By the time Beatrice came to me for help, she was ready to cut every single person out of her life so that she could have some peace. I asked Beatrice about how she was feeling about the world around her. She told me that people were jerks. She said she had learned to be careful in life because all anyone ever wanted was to "take, take, take."

"Ah ha!" I said. "You've found your pattern. Now you know where to start looking!" She was, of course, not that excited. She didn't yet understand how finding the pattern was such a big key to revealing her Soul Contracts and discovering her Divine Light within.

Beatrice's pattern was to help everyone around her. She always found great networking opportunities for others, assisted them with their business, watched their pets, and listened to their problems—but she never asked for or expected anything back. In her experience, she had found that most people wouldn't come through; and besides, even if they *did* come through, she could never ask for help because she didn't want to put anyone out. Based on what she had identified as her repeating pattern of helping everyone without asking or expecting anything back, I pressed Beatrice to decipher what Soul Contract could be causing the negative pattern.

After some thought, she told me she believed her Soul Contract was that she must earn the love of others by doing things for them and giving to them. In one short conversation, Beatrice easily identified one of her related Soul Contracts: "Give to others in order to receive love." As she continued to look at her Soul System, she discovered other Soul Contracts embedded within her Root Belief System. They were related to vulnerability ("I must prevent myself from feeing unsafe"), shunning love ("I give too much to avoid the disappointment of not receiving anything back"), and other beliefs.

Take a moment to look at the specific areas in your life where you feel uncomfortable. Is it your finances? Career? Love? Self-worth?

Addiction? Look for the repeating pattern. That will be your first glorious clue to learning what your most pressing block is made of!

Method 3: Unrelated Clues

Another way to be aware of your Soul Contracts is by going through the back door. This is a little trickier than the first two techniques, but if you can use this method, you'll actually get more information about yourself.

By this time, you know that contracts are most likely blocking you in more than one area. Sometimes, when you're searching for your Soul Contracts, you may find unrelated clues that allow you to go deeper. Using these clues, you may realize that you have more than one contract blocking you or that the contract blocking you is different from what you thought! For example, I've met people who thought they had a block around money, but when they used this method to look deeper, they learned that the block was actually related to *all* types of support.

When you find that you have one Soul Contract, don't forget to check for others. Soul Contracts tend to travel in groups within our Root Belief Systems. This is because we are very thorough! We try to take control of our lives and stop ourselves from re-experiencing our Seed Thoughts, rather than trusting in our inner brilliance and light.

Let's look at my client Terry as an example. Terry came to me because she felt that she had a block in weight loss. She was working out five times a week, going to ballroom dancing sessions, and trying to eat better—yet her weight wasn't really changing. In our first session, Terry was frustrated because I wasn't interested in the long list of products and programs she had tried for losing weight. She wanted to tell me the whole story about her weight loss—but that story didn't matter; it was the story she *wasn't* telling that was the key to her Soul Contract.

To begin, I asked Terry to describe her workouts. She told me she worked out through a program on the internet that she found motivating because the host of the program was very fit and enthusiastic. When I asked Terry to describe a typical workout, she said it was usually three to five rounds of different exercises. Then she posted her scores on the site's Facebook page. Terry mentioned that she was confused when she looked at the page: For most people, the number of reps per round decreased as the intervals progressed, but for her, the number of reps increased after each round. Her last round was usually the round with the most reps.

I pushed Terry to talk more about this odd pattern. Logic said that as her body got tired, the number of reps she did should decrease. As she talked, Terry realized that she wouldn't push herself as hard during the first few rounds. She was concerned about having enough energy for the end of the workout. I asked her if this pattern appeared in any other areas of her life—holding back, in case she needed more for later.

She exclaimed, "Oh my God! That is how I am with money. I never want to spend it because I'm worried that I won't have enough later!" Then, after some more thought, she realized she did the same thing with the minutes on her phone. Even though she never came close to going over her wireless plan, she still counted each minute, reasoning that you never know what could happen.

Terry discovered that this pattern affected more areas of her life. First she found that she held back at the grocery store. She didn't know how much space she might need in her cart, so even if she was only buying a few things, she squished them against the side of the cart, just in case. She held back with her friends as well. She didn't want to use up all the help from her friends (in her mind it was limited), so she would wait until she was completely desperate before reaching out.

She was even able to find the pattern in her health. Terry suffered from thyroid problems that made her feel very tired all the time. Because of this, she never gave 100 percent physically, since she didn't know if she was going to need her energy later. Terry had finally discovered her Soul Contract. Best of all, she identified it by looking at seemingly unrelated areas in her life. The block showed up in her body, work, exercise routine, and relationships.

You may be saying to yourself, "Yeah, but my block is only in my relationship with women" or "Not me—it's just my career that's blocked." I encourage you to look deeper than that. Can you find your block in other areas—perhaps manifesting more subtly? Where in your career are you blocked? Do you tend to work for uncaring bosses who expect you to come through, no matter what? Does that description sound like anyone else in your life? How does that pattern apply to your home life? Does your family expect you to make miracles happen, just because you've pulled them off before? Look for common ground. A totally unrelated piece could turn out to be the key to identifying at least one of your Lifetime Soul Contracts.

Method 4: Exercise to Reveal Your Soul Contracts

Some people like to use an exercise to figure out their contracts. With that in mind, get two pieces of paper and a pencil or pen. If you are a typer like me and would rather write on the computer, that is fine. You just need to be able to record what you want to say.

Next, you're going to write, about two paragraphs in all. You may be gung ho to figure out your Soul Contracts, but overwriting will take away from the effectiveness of what you are about to do—so will underwriting. For the sake of accuracy and clarity, stick to two paragraphs.

In the first paragraph, describe yourself. Write at the top of the paragraph: How I Describe Myself to Others. Pretend that someone is interviewing you and you need to tell them what kind of person you are. What makes you special? Do you have certain behaviors? Thoughts? What do you do for a job? What do you really value about yourself? Spend a few minutes writing this first paragraph. Perhaps you want to say the words out loud and then write them down—whatever works. Be honest in your description and imagine you really are sharing it with another person.

On the next sheet of paper or at the top of the second paragraph, write: Areas in Which I Am Unfulfilled. Write about the areas of your life where you feel things are not going the way you want. You could write things like, "I always feel like I'm not working hard enough at my job," "I never have enough money to go on vacation," or "I feel like the world is against me." Whatever comes to mind, write it down. The reality is that you already know what areas make you feel less than, so allow yourself time and space to think, feel, and write about them.

Once you have done this, sit quietly for a couple of minutes. If you feel these paragraphs are complete, you're ready to start the next step in the exercise. But don't move on until you've taken the time to ensure you're completely satisfied with what you have written.

Now, take a look at the list where you described the type of person you are and compare it to the list of unfulfilling areas of your life. This comparison will likely help you figure out at least one of your Lifetime Soul Contracts. Most people unknowingly create what they believe are positive personality traits based on their Soul Contracts.

For example, a person with a Soul Contract that states they must prove their worth to the world will often describe themselves as very responsible or intelligent. They say they can figure out problems no one else can. A person whose Soul Contract says, "I must control everything to feel safe" may describe themselves as organized, dependable, and in control of all situations. It's incredible how ingrained these Soul Contracts can be. They can run so deep that the person carrying them has no idea that the Soul Contracts are not really who they are.

Let's say you wrote down, "I'm a great friend to everyone around me. I help people, even when they don't realize they need help. Everyone can depend on me and I'm always reliable." Now, to identify a Soul Contract, look at the other paragraph. Most likely something in that second writing says you feel like no one is there for you. You feel alone in the world. When you put these ideas together, you will see that they are actually one and the same. The words you wrote are red flags pointing exactly to the area you need to look at. In this example, you would need to look at both giving and receiving in your relationships to determine what your Soul Contracts are.

Being a good friend or wanting to be successful in your career are not blocks on their own. Many people perform these actions naturally, and that's a wonderful thing. They are connected to their brilliance; out of that connection, they can enjoy helping others or finding fulfillment at work. For our purposes, though, it's the way these actions correspond to a type of need (i.e., "I need to be the best in order to feel good about myself," or "I need to be a good friend so others will see that I really am a good person") that is important. I've worked with many clients who pride themselves on being giving, loving people. Everyone around them feels gratitude for their work. However, when they start looking more deeply at themselves, they realize their generosity is intended to alleviate pain. As long as the pain is there, Soul Contracts will continue to thwart those positive actions and drive down their vibration.

Continue to compare the two paragraphs. Put them side-by-side in front of you and search for clues. The reality is that your goodness, wholeness, happiness, fulfillment, peace, purity, and support from the world don't depend on what job you have, what acts you perform, how other people feel about you, how organized you are, or anything else. They are part of the universal support system that is naturally part of your life—when you believe in your light and discover your inner brilliance.

You are a beautiful Soul no matter what decisions you've made throughout your lifetimes. Soul Contracts, Root Belief Systems, Seed Thoughts—these all cover up your light within, but as you master and release each one, you'll find the divinity inside you. So use the two paragraphs to discover where you're compensating for not believing in your inner divinity. You'll find that it's much easier to reveal your Soul Contract and see what is *really* getting in your way.

When you do get a handle on at least one of your Lifetime Soul Contracts, it might be a tremendous epiphany that hits you all at once. The discovery of the contract could also show up as many small ah-ha moments; that is fine too. Any way you become aware of your contract is the perfect way for you. Your insights, whatever size, will assist you.

If you've taken the time to do the exercise, it is a good sign that you're also willing to do the deep work that comes in the next step— exposing your Seed Thoughts. If you didn't fully commit to this exercise and said to yourself, "How much can I really learn about myself from writing two paragraphs?" that's understandable, but it probably indicates that you should not move on to the next step.

Spend some time working in the awareness step. Really look at yourself, your behaviors, and the choices behind them—even those little nagging thoughts in the back of your head that you've never told anyone before. All those things are the ticket to finding your Soul Contracts and discovering what is really motivating you. You can do this, but first you must be committed to doing the work.

7

Step 2: Awareness II

Hopefully, you're excited at this point about your newfound awareness. You've found some of the Soul Contracts that direct your life without your knowledge. You have a good feel for the various blocks they are creating. With all this information, you are in a position to reveal the underlying Seed Thoughts, which will allow you to expose the lesson. You can learn the reason this system came into existence in the first place. What Seed Thought led you to create this Soul Contract in the beginning? Once you have identified the Seed Thought, figuring out the lesson behind it is often very easy.

Identifying the Seed Thought—which is what the Soul Contract anchors to—is the only effective way to reach the mastery step in the Soul System process. In order to reach mastery, you have to know what lesson you need to learn. Saying, "I have blocks around making worthwhile friends. They always leave me hanging when I need them most," or saying, "I have Soul Contracts around money because I always lose it," will not lead you to achieve true mastery. You can't just want to release these contracts—you have to explore the *why* behind the block. Working on your blocks without this knowledge will only allow you to work superficially.

Four Steps to Identifying Your Seed Thoughts & Lessons

Most people find that this phase of working with your Soul System is like a *Rocky* montage. Picture Sylvester Stallone running up the steps in front of the Philadelphia Museum of Art, jogging with his trainer beside him and punching a speed bag, all while "Eye of the Tiger" plays in the background. The clips show all his hard work and dedication once he fully commits himself to the work of winning. Keep that example in mind as you begin this step. When you fully dedicate yourself, you'll find the most success. It's time for you to do everything you can and use every resource in your power to seek out all the different places this Seed Thought rears its ugly head. The more places you can find the Seed Thought, the easier it will be to figure out what you were supposed to learn while you were creating this system in the first place.

One last note: your Seed Thoughts aren't always what you expect. I had one client who was adopted. She thought her Seed Thought formed from feeling not good enough when her biological mother gave her to the adoption agency. As she investigated further, she figured out that her Seed Thought *I'm no good* stemmed from a conversation she overheard between two of the nuns in the orphanage; they said since her mother was a run-around, loose type of girl, she would probably turn out that way as well. If what you turn up doesn't make sense at first, don't let that deter you.

Now you're ready to harness a deeper awareness. As I've already said, your Soul Contract couldn't exist without the Seed Thought anchoring it to create a Root Belief System. In this chapter, we're going to decipher the Seed Thought (the beginning of it all!), which will allow you to see the lesson, master the Seed Thought, and release it.

Exposing the Seed Thought is like searching for the *why* behind your Soul Contracts. Simply put, you're trying to understand what emotion or thought drove you to put that Soul Contract in place to begin with. The emotions (called Discordant Emotions) and thoughts you discover are actually your Seed Thoughts; they are the root of your block.

Step One: Identify the Moment

The goal in this step is to put to use the work you just did in identifying your Soul Contracts. Look at one of the Soul Contracts you just identified and think of a specific past experience in your life when this contract has shown up. This is called identifying the moment, and it is this moment that you'll use to work with the resulting feelings, ideas, and emotions driving you in the following steps. Keep that experience in mind as you follow the next three steps.

Step Two: Record the Feelings and Thoughts

Now it's time to understand what is happening emotionally when your contracts are influencing you. Just before the event occurred, how were you feeling? During the event, how were you feeling? What were you thinking? Answer honestly. Do not give a vague "I was fine." Spend time and energy really looking into your emotions and processing them. Write everything in your journal. For example, as you struggled to tell your friend you couldn't take her to the airport because you were sick, or you fought with your older sister over who would drive the car, what were you feeling? Were you worried your friend would hate you? Were you concerned that your sister wasn't going to be able to follow directions and get to your destination on time (like always)? Were you feeling that your friend deserved a ride to the airport?

Your mind can conjure up some complicated thoughts and emotions about the simple events in your past. Paying attention to those thoughts and emotions—what they really are, even if it isn't politically correct—is the key to understanding the Seed Thought. Keep track of these emotions and thoughts. Your best bet will be to write them down in a small notebook. Do not write too much, and keep your words simple. For example, you could write, "Driving Dawn to the airport—felt like she worked hard and deserved it." Do not complicate your journal with extra sentences. The simpler your information is, the easier it will be to do the next step.

Step Three: Identify the Seed Thought

Do not read this step until you have finished recording all your thoughts and feelings.

You've now diligently examined at least one event in your life where one of your Soul Contracts showed up. Now it's time to do some detective work. Take a look at your journal. What do you see? Start looking for a pattern in your behavior, emotions, and thinking. Stay objective as you hunt and read through your journal, as if you were reading a textbook. The more objective you can be, the easier this step will be. Did you use the same word or phrase several times? Pay attention to what you wrote. Your emotions and thoughts will give you clues about what you need to learn.

The pattern that emerges will be a repeating negative emotion and thought. Look for the unexpressed feeling you had each time you noticed you were experiencing the Soul Contract block—but also look for feelings and emotions you were trying to avoid each time the Soul Contract affected you. These will provide great clues. When Dawn asked you for a ride to the airport, and you determined that she deserved the ride more than you deserved to stay home and rest, you were also expressing that you didn't deserve to be made a priority. The underlying feeling (or Seed Thought) in this example would most likely be *I'm not deserving* or *I'm not worthy* or *I'm not good enough*. By picking apart your emotional experience, your motivation will be made clear. The Seed Thought's corresponding Discordant Emotions may be anxiety, fear, nervousness, and disappointment.

The following exercise will help you further develop the patterns you're beginning to notice:

1. First, write the pattern you have observed in your journal. This may be only one or two sentences. Don't complicate it. The simpler, the better. For the airport example, your note might be, "Noticed that I feel I haven't done well enough to deserve to stay home and relax."
2. Second, rewrite that sentence as a fear without the detail. So, in this example, you would write something like, "I fear that I have not done enough to deserve anything in return."
3. Now, take that sentence and simplify it even more. In this case, the sentence would be something like, "I fear I'm not good enough."

Take note of the repeating emotions that accompany the Seed Thought you've just identified. Those are actually the Discordant Emotions you buried in your Soul along with the Seed Thought.

Step Four: Identify the Lesson

Phew! Now that you are aware of your Seed Thought, you can move on to identifying the lesson. Luckily, you'll find that, after all your hard work, determining the lesson is the easiest step in this whole book!

We are beings of perfection, beauty, truth, and light—beings of the Universe. Any thought that tells us we are anything other than that is false. Therefore, whatever your Seed Thought is, the lesson is to begin acting, behaving, and living the exact opposite—to believe in the brilliance of your Soul.

I'm not good enough becomes *I am 100 percent good.*

I'm not worthy becomes *I am worthy of all* and *I'm as worthy as everyone else.*

I'm not safe becomes *I am protected by God, Source, or Universe and all of my friends and support system.*

We will cover how to learn these lessons at the Soul level in the following chapters. But until then, be happy! You've empowered yourself. You have identified the Seed Thought you were dealing with when you originally created your Soul Contract. This decreases the power of the Soul Contract greatly—simply reaching this point in the process, you'll find that the Soul Contract already has less influence in your life than it did when you first began.

It is incredible to me how many people have tried to do their Soul Contract work without stopping to figure out their Seed Thought, Discordant Emotions, and lessons. I recently spoke at a popular online teleseminar in which I gave the audience the gift of a free group clearing around their Soul Contracts. While most of the people who received the clearing were grateful, one woman wrote me an email that said, "Danielle, I have done many techniques to get things shifting in my life, including your Soul Contracts clearing prayer. Still—no luck whatsoever. I have not met the man of my dreams yet. I feel like I have been on the verge forever, and yet nothing is happening!"

With just that sentence, it was immediately clear to me that this woman hadn't yet addressed her Seed Thoughts and the deep, helpful work they create. (And remember, working with your Soul System is a permanent change, not a snap-your-fingers type of fix.) What this woman didn't understand is that it's impossible to clear any Soul Contract without first learning and embodying the lesson that contract is in place to teach. In that teleseminar, I had explained to the listeners that the only contracts that would actually release through the clearing were those they had already worked on by identifying the underlying Seed Thoughts, finding the lesson and embodying it. So no matter how hard you try, you *must* do the underlying work. There are no shortcuts.

A client named Claire came to me expecting her block to be cleared immediately. She said, "I know what my block is: I always pick the wrong guy. I want you to clear that for me." Claire complained that every man she met and fell for quickly left her. She recounted story after story in which each seemingly wonderful man wooed her, but within a month of sleeping with him, he left her. She felt unloved when she wanted nothing more than to be loved. She told me she had tried various techniques for finding love, none of which worked.

According to Claire, the only challenge she had in her life was love. However, Seed Thoughts permeate your entire existence. In this case, Claire was missing the big picture. She believed her Soul Contracts were limited to love and made men leave her. Claire had done some research into my work, and when I suggested that we look deeper to find out why she had created her current Soul Contracts, she quipped, "I just want you to remove the Soul Contracts of eternal love, chastity, and loneliness, so I can get on with it. I just want to find Mr. Right and get married, already." The problem here was that Claire was missing the entire point: the Soul Contract release comes at the end, after you have learned the lesson and begun letting go of your Seed Thoughts. Otherwise, it's like trying to put the cart before the horse—you're not going to get anywhere.

Why did Claire put these Soul Contracts into her life in the first place? What Seed Thought was she experiencing to make her decide enough is enough? It's easy to identify the Soul Contracts from clearly repeated negative patterns or blocks—but that is where Claire had stopped. It's more important and harder to figure out why the Seed Thoughts and contracts were there in the first place.

When I met with Claire, rather than listing out the areas in which she was blocked, I decided that she should look at the situations where the Soul Contracts influenced her. I've found this method to be very helpful when a client resists or struggles to see how their pattern shows up throughout their life (rather than in just one area). Since Claire was sure that the only place her pattern occurred was in her relationships with men, we looked at that area first.

We delved into each relationship. Quickly, a pattern began to emerge. Claire learned that the men she chose were not good communicators. In fact, they tended to be silent and brooding. Claire's father didn't take much notice of her, which meant that she felt like she had to try harder to get her boyfriends' attention, hold their interest, and make them communicate. As Claire looked at her past relationships, it became clear that she believed that she had to earn love; she had believed this since she was very young. Claire remembered countless times where she bent over backward to meet a man's needs, hoping that her generosity would open them up—just like she'd behaved with her father, she remembered. In the end, it didn't work. The man would grow tired of Claire's doting ways and leave her.

Claire's underlying belief that she wasn't worthy of love was creating havoc in her love life as well as in other areas, such as her career. She began to see that she also needed to overwork herself to get credit for what she did at her job. She had to go to great lengths for her friends, as well, in order to be a good friend. Once she identified this as the Seed Thought that her Soul Contracts were anchored to, she was able to move forward in her Soul System work. But she couldn't do any of that until she knew the Seed Thought. For Claire, identifying her Seed Thought was the missing link.

Remember, it's wonderful to identify what your Soul Contracts are, but in the end, it's all about the lesson, which you'll figure out once you know your Seed Thought. Your struggle is not a punishment. It's a way to help you believe in the beauty of who you are.

Extra Help: Changing Lenses

As children, we don't have many choices. Think about being five years old. If your parents were fighting, you couldn't leave the house or go somewhere else. If you didn't like how your mother was treating you or what happened when your father was around, there wasn't much you could do about it. You could remain quiet. You could tell an adult that you were unhappy. However, most children don't have the sophisticated communication skills or the emotional maturity to do those things. As a child, you really didn't have many options. You had to figure life out and make decisions about how to handle it to the best of your ability. For many of us, that meant aligning ourselves with another person (usually a parent) so deeply that we let go of our true sense of self. Some people will reclaim their sense of self during their rebellious teenage years, while others will continue feeling lost into their thirties or forties—sometimes for the rest of their lives!

When I met my client Julie, she had a very successful career as a senior manager in the tech field. She had a husband and two kids, spent quite a bit of time with her mother, and had a small group of close friends. But Julie felt unhappy, unloved, and dissatisfied.

As Julie described her life to me, it was obvious that she couldn't figure out why she didn't feel loved or happy. On paper, she had all the ingredients for what our society terms a happy, successful life. In fact, it took Julie years to seek help because she felt she was being selfish by wanting more from her life. When Julie mentioned that her mother was coming for a weekend visit, my psychic antennae went up. I asked her if that was a good thing, and she said emphatically, "Yes! Of course it is! I love my mom!" As she described what a major part of her life her mom was, I was buzzing. Something more was going on.

When I pressed her, Julie confessed that she didn't really remember a lot from her childhood. She only knew it was kind of challenging. She'd heard stories from her mom, but her own memories felt lacking because she couldn't recall the things that her mother talked about. She told me that her mom was always mentioning something from the past, and Julie told me how sad she felt that she couldn't remember those things. I explained to Julie that it felt to me like she had decided at a very young age to adopt her mother's version of reality as her own in order to survive. This would allow young Julie to gain a sense of safety, security, and love.

Julie's answer? "Absolutely not! My mother was and is an amazing woman! I mean, I know she had a hard time raising me when I was little, but that's because I was such a difficult child. She did everything she could to handle me! My mother really is the best mother I've ever seen."

As children, we all develop a method for interacting with the world. Those methods are strongly influenced by the people in our lives and the care we do (or don't) receive at that time. Many Soul Contracts are created in our very early years—usually around three to five years old. As we grow up, we come to believe that those Soul Contracts actually make up the people that we are. Julie, for example, had created Soul Contracts that pushed her to manage everyone around her while keeping them at a distance. She didn't risk feeling disappointed when other people didn't come through. But in our sessions, she struggled to understand how any of this could have stemmed from her mother's parenting.

I often work with clients who have few memories from childhood. Most people were in similar situations to Julie's: they had become very close with their mother (or father), and they were extremely understanding of their parent's past behavior. Many people who are in this situation don't realize that there are Soul Contracts at work. Additionally, they don't appreciate that in order to accept this perspective from their caretaker, they actually had to push away the authentic emotions they were experiencing at the time. Discordant Emotions, made up of buried emotions, continue to resurface over the years, adding fuel to the Seed Thought fire, often causing the person to create more and more Soul Contracts to keep them buried.

To understand why you put these Soul Contracts in place, start differentiating your own memories and experiences from those belonging to the people around you. You must start using your own lens, rather than the lens of the person you overidentified with in childhood. Now, this does not mean you should reject a parent or particular caregiver; you need to reject the lens they handed you all those years ago. As an adult, it is impossible to understand yourself when your sense of self comes from the people around you rather than from your own experience. This means going back through the stories you've heard about your childhood and working to understand them through what *you* were feeling (or might have felt, based on your adult knowledge of yourself). Find your own interpretation.

Julie grew up believing that she was a very unruly, uncontrollable child, who tortured her little sister. There was a particular story that she had heard over and over that always made her feel guilty. Her mother told her that when Julie was eight and her younger sister was five, Julie handed her sister a glass candy cane and told her that it was real. When her little sister bit down on it, the glass cracked and cut the inside of her mouth; she needed three stitches. I asked Julie to re-examine the story. Did she ever recall intentionally setting out to torture her sister? The emotions it would take to do that would be anger, revenge, or violence of some kind. Did she ever recall feeling that way? I asked if she currently experienced those feelings in her life. Her answer was no.

Julie realized that she had accepted her mom's reality as her own. Applying her mom's lens to her own life gave a very different view of what she had experienced. Basically, at the Soul level, her mom said, "If we look through life with this lens, it shows that I was a good mom. This lens makes it so that I can feel good about what I've done. I can accept the decisions I made. If you accept this lens, we can be very close. You will feel safe, secure, and loved by me."

Julie's mom didn't create this lens because she was a bad person. She wasn't trying to hurt Julie or manipulate her; she had her own struggles. The reality she gave Julie was truly her own reality. Julie's current challenge was that she hadn't let go of the lens her mother gave her. She was deeply afraid that if she differentiated from her mother, she would lose her.

I asked Julie to think about the candy cane story. If revenge and violence weren't part of her repertoire of feelings now, they probably weren't part of her emotions then—so what could she have been feeling? As Julie let go of the story she had been told by her mother, she imagined what had really been in her mind. She told me how her sister had been sick since birth; their parents spent most of their time and energy trying to make her sister better. Julie remembered feeling like no one was paying attention to her and wanting to make everyone laugh. As she sat with this story, it slowly turned into a memory. She just wanted to get a good laugh out of the family (including her sister) and had simply miscalculated. She hadn't known what biting a glass candy cane could do to a person's mouth.

Julie had a huge breakthrough when she began exploring her own lens. She translated more of her mother's stories into her own reality. For stories that she wasn't able to adapt into her own memory, she could speculate about what had actually happened based on the new view of herself as a child. She realized she was still harboring the Discordant Emotions of jealousy (over the attention her sister received), disappointment (that she didn't get as much attention), and sadness (because she truly wanted the love she wasn't getting). The more she worked, the more she realized that she had every right to view her life through her own lens. It didn't make her a bad daughter or a selfish person—in fact, it allowed her to see who she was and understand why she made the decisions she did. She finally understood the lesson behind her Seed Thoughts: she was just as worthy as the next person of having her own life, experiences, and support.

The Discordant Emotions that Julie experienced in her adult life turned out to be the exact same feelings that she had when she was three and contracted to take her mother's reality on as her own. She had buried those emotions deep within her Soul. As she delved into the memories, Julie was not only working with those old Seed Thoughts, but was also able to release that long-buried negative energy.

As a child, all you want is the love of your caretakers. You're going to do whatever you can to create a loving situation—even if it means ignoring your own reality, emotions, and actions in order to take on someone else's. This is actually a very normal part of growing up. The problem is that this often happens at the Soul level, and thirty or fifty years later, you're still following the same pattern for safety, security, and love. At some point, you have to let go of those old patterns and create new ones based on your light, your adult point of view, and all that you have experienced since childhood.

It's important to spend time looking back at your early childhood. I've found that most Seed Thoughts are planted in early years, between the ages of three to five. Soul Contracts are added a little later, during years six to ten. You may find that you need to separate your reality from that of a caretaker or loved one before you can begin working with your Soul System. If your memories are easily accessible, however, you can start working from there.

A word of caution: if you have memories, be sure they are yours! Sometimes another person's reality is so ingrained in you that you don't realize you don't have your own memories! Do you really remember a certain experience, or has the story just been told so many times that you think it's your reality? Many people think their memories are intact, only to find out that they were stories told by a family member. If this is the case for you, releasing the other person's lens will be just as beneficial as it is for someone who can't access their memories at all.

It is impossible to view your life through your own lens if you are emotionally activated every time you think of your past. Without your own perspective, how can you have a bird's-eye view of your life and figure out your Soul Contracts and Seed Thoughts?

To really look at your past, differentiate yourself from your caretaker, and learn your childhood's important lessons, you have to unplug your energy from what happened. Once you have done that, you'll find that the memory will not feel as intense. In fact, your newly objective eye will give you freedom to understand what really happened at that moment—which will, in turn, allow you to learn from it and move forward.

8

Step 3: Embody the Lesson

It's time to work on getting the lesson behind your current Soul-
level challenge. At this point, you're probably looking at yourself in
a very different way. In this step, we take advantage of that. You'll see
changes start to show up in bits and pieces in your world.

Intellectual understanding is the result of research, classes, trying new tools and techniques, reading books, talking with friends,
and more. It is an outwardly focused way of functioning, and it
results in a lot of knowledge—not much of which is practical. I've
worked with many people who did not realize they were playing the
role of the perpetual student—absorbing all the spiritual and self-
help information out there, but not advancing in life. It's great to
learn all about how energy works or how to talk with your Guides
or what your Seed Thoughts and contracts are—but if you don't take
action, this information is worthless.

In Soul System work, awareness and understanding can only open
your eyes to what is going on. You could spend years researching

this stuff. You could come live with me as my student, but until you shifted yourself out of perpetual-student mode and moved into action mode, you would not make the deep, Soul-level shifts you are looking for. To embody the lesson, you are going to have to feel. You're also going to have to get dirty and take risks. Your emotions may get messy—and perhaps you'll even lose yourself for a while. That's as it should be. It's not about looking at how your Soul System functions from the outside—it's about feeling how it functions within you. That's the embodiment you are looking for. We're not using microscopes to understand how life comes together—you know that! We're getting down and dirty, picking up the yuck, tasting life, spitting out what we don't like, and becoming one with what works. This is true embodiment. So get ready to *feel*, experience, and really live this stuff. It's part of your life now—so no microscopes, no more school. Just bring your true, authentic self to the table.

Freedom From the Past

An attachment to the past can stand in the way of embodying your lesson. If you are reminded that your history is plagued with failure every time you think about finally being able to make money or freeing yourself from being so critical, you will struggle more with the upcoming work. Most of all, you want to be able to look at events in your life. You want to properly release your past so that you can learn from it, rather than be held back.

If you re-experience emotional turmoil whenever you think of your childhood—that incident in school or the time your family went bankrupt—how can you get true perspective on your past? You can use an energetic exercise I call the "bubble disconnect" to move into a beautiful, calm, objective place regarding those difficult moments.

When you can be objective, you'll entertain different viewpoints, new ideas, and perhaps even rediscover your own experience in a completely fresh way. Rediscovery is a normal part of the release process, but it may be difficult to achieve. The bubble disconnect tool will allow you to revisit the past and defuse it from your old perspective (bogged down by Seed Thoughts) and your new one (as you continue to address your Seed Thoughts). In turn, you'll be open to learning the lessons embedded within these difficult moments.

EXERCISE: THE BUBBLE DISCONNECT

Begin this exercise by finding a quiet space where you feel calm and can take time for yourself.

1. Call On Your Guides

Call on your Spiritual Guides for assistance. If you are not so inclined, just sit and feel calm. If you are someone who enjoys working with Guides, angels, and spirits, imagine that they are with you, ready to assist you. If you're unsure how to do this, simply say, "I am now calling on my Guides of 100 percent Divine Light to assist me with this work today." Do what feels comfortable and helps create a calm, safe, secure moment.

2. Choose Your Event or Experience

Pick an experience from your past that is related to the Seed Thought you've chosen to work on. Ideally, once you have removed the energetic attachment to that experience, you will be able to understand and embody the lesson behind the Seed Thought. Which experience from your past should you pick? For your first time, choose a very specific experience. Think small. In the beginning, you should go experience by experience.

The best event to choose for this first round is something specific that still gets your goat. I have a client in Australia, for example, whose husband tends to nag and disrespect her. Once, he started picking on her about the way she cut her meat. He told her she was strange, that she didn't know how to do anything right, and that people were going to laugh at her because of her table manners. This would be a great incident for this client to choose for the bubble disconnect exercise. It was a specific event, her emotions were strong and present when she remembered it, and it's related to her Seed Thought *I'm not good enough*. Stay away from choosing a general topic, such as your mother or an ongoing power struggle, and look for specific experiences instead. You can use this technique for larger, ongoing issues in the future, but you must first master it at the simplest level. The event that you choose should also involve you and one significant person in your life.

Next, draw on your childlike tendencies and get into five-year-old-kid mode. If you take the next few steps too seriously, you won't benefit from the work. Hop around, do some jumping jacks—whatever you can so that you're not sitting still, overanalyzing yourself until you can't move.

3. Construct Your Bubble

Imagine that the person who is involved in your chosen event (just one person) is standing across the room, about ten feet away. Notice how they stand, what they are wearing, and even the emotional sense you get from them. Allow that person to be present for a moment.

Next, imagine that you are putting that person inside a bubble. The bubble easily accommodates the person and envelops them lovingly. Continue to visualize the bubble with the person inside it across the room. Know that you are safe, secure, and loved as you create this through your imagination. What you are about to do with this bubble is for the greatest and highest good of everyone involved. Stay calm and focused.

Some people worry about placing someone else inside a bubble. Remember that the bubble is full of love, created to help both you and the other person release energies that are no longer assisting you. The only intention here is balance, truth, release, and clarity.

4. Add Emotion

This is one of the most critical steps in the process. The intention of this step is to uncover the buried emotion and related energy linked with the memory of this event. As long as that energy is hidden within your memory, it will continue to act as a silent power source. It will keep fueling your emotions and taking away your ability to look at the memory objectively so you can learn from it and move on.

So, let's work on removing the power source. This can be difficult since you've covered it up with emotions, behaviors, contracts, and more. We're going to start releasing by looking toward those emotions. For the next two to three minutes you are going to be uncomfortable. That's it—only two to three minutes. If you avoid the discomfort, you will not find the positive outcome on the other side. You can have an immediate, powerful experience in this step by allowing yourself a little—or perhaps a lot—of discomfort as you work. Think of it this way—the two minutes will free you to enjoy the lifetime of change you'll have once you can understand and embody the lesson behind the experience.

While imagining your chosen person in the bubble across the room, begin to think about the memory you've chosen. Don't think about it like you would tell a story to a friend. For this to work, you have to go into the emotions. So, rather than telling yourself, "I was really mad at Ralph when he did that," ask yourself how the anger really feels. Spend time locating the emotion within yourself. Bring it forward until you are no longer thinking about the anger; you are *feeling* it. You are experiencing your anger. You may notice that you are balling your fists or tensing your body. You may feel tingles on the back of your neck. Whatever your sign for anger is, find it. Imagine that your anger is filling up a huge beach ball in your chest. Keep filling that beach ball with all that anger you feel. Close your eyes if it helps you concentrate.

Once you have filled yourself with all the anger you can gather, it's time to take the next step. Using your hands, lift the imaginary beach ball filled with your negative emotion and place it inside the big bubble with the person. As you do, it sinks to the bottom of the bubble. Take a moment to notice how much of the bubble is now filled with the negative emotion. Does it take up a quarter of the bubble? An eighth? Your goal is to keep doing this exercise until you have filled that bubble completely to the top.

I used the emotion of anger only as an example. You may not find that anger is the first, strongest emotion you can pull up. You may start with embarrassment, fear, or disgust; anger or despair could come up later. Choose a different emotion to fill each beach ball. You'll probably find that you can fill the bubble with more than one emotion.

The most important aspect of this step is being *in* the emotion, not thinking about the emotion. I've seen many people who can talk about a horrible experience they had without batting an eye. They recount the details, but do everything they can to avoid going back into the energy of the experience. If you do this, ask yourself, "But how did it *feel*?" over and over again. Get back into that buried energy. If you cannot access those emotions, you may want to choose a different event or person (or both) related to your Seed Thought until you get better at accessing those memories.

By bringing up the emotions, you might discover things that you are embarrassed to admit—even to yourself! This is healthy and proves how deeply you are working. Allow yourself to purge all the emotions, feelings, and ideas around that one particular situation. Make every effort to be emotionally honest and present with your memory. Many people buried these negative energies because they determined that what they really felt at the time was not OK, not politically correct, or unfair. This is your chance to release all that. No one else will ever know.

As you move to the next step, know that the two to three minutes you spent filling the beach balls were the hardest part of the whole exercise. Phew!

5. Find the Connection

Once you have completely filled the bubble, you are ready to move on to the next step. Filling the bubble doesn't necessarily mean that you have exhausted the emotions you buried, but it does mean you have done all you could in this particular bubble disconnect session.

Next, use your imagination to look at the completely filled bubble. It is probably not a light, bright, airy bubble anymore. It is filled with so much negativity. Most people see the bubble as heavy, dark, and gross. And why shouldn't it be? Negativity is dark, heavy, slimy, and gunky—like tar. You've just worked to pull this out of yourself and deposit it into the bubble.

Imagine that there is a cord attached to the bubble. You have fed your energy into the situation through this cord. Your Seed Thought powers the negativity you send through the cord into this negative memory! This cord is comprised 100 percent of your own energy—not the energy of the other person or the energy of the experience, but *your own energy*. There is no blame in this situation, only claiming responsibility. You've been powering the negative emotions around this situation for years. It's time to claim your part, break the connection, and move forward. Your job right now is to work on disconnecting.

As you learned in chapter 5, people are happier and clearer when their energy is grounded in their core. Energy that leaves us in a cord, like the energy you see in the bubble disconnect exercise, is certainly not grounded. It is time to take back this ungrounded, negative energy that has fed this situation for years. You're going to shift it. Begin by noticing if the cord extends from the bubble to a particular place on your body. Does it attach to your belly button area? Your heart? Your right shoulder? Perhaps it splits and attaches to you in two or more spots. Take a moment to notice this; it is very important.

If you're having trouble imagining the cord connecting to you, do a quick imagination exercise. Think of a blue turtle. Think of a red dinosaur. Think of a loud thunderclap. Now, go back to using your imagination to decipher where the cord is fixed on your body. Don't forget to spend a few moments noticing the quality of the cord. In a healthy situation, it might be light, sparkly, and almost transparent. Pure energy would be zooming back and forth, almost undetectable. Most likely, however, the cord you are now seeing is heavy, like an umbilical cord. Perhaps it has mold or vines growing on it. Perhaps it's inflexible or made of steel. Let your imagination run wild so that you can really see what your cord is like. Write your impressions in your journal so that you don't forget them. You'll test this work later.

6. Disconnect & Reclaim

Use your imagination to see the dark, gross bubble hovering across the room from you. It's as thick, heavy, and icky as ever. In your mind's eye or physically (whichever works better for you), reach your hand over to the bubble. Gently grab where it meets the cord and take hold of that imaginary cord. Do this with love. Pull the cord out of the bubble, like pulling the plug out of an electrical wall socket. You may even imagine hearing a pop as it releases from the bubble.

A word about pulling out the cord: you've worked hard on this. You chose an event and person that still have the power to affect you emotionally. Perhaps this person is still part of your life. When you pull this cord out of the bubble, you aren't pulling the cord on the relationship. You are not sending the person out of your life or banning them from ever speaking with you again. You are only reclaiming the energy that you were using to feed negativity into your memory. That's it. The person inside the bubble will not feel pain because you unplugged. In fact, doing this exercise may provide the person in the bubble an unexpected opportunity for growth.

So what do you do now that you're standing there with the cord hanging in your hand? Reclaim your energy, that's what! Start gathering the imaginary energy cord in your hands. Wad up as much of it as you can. This is your energy—energy which has not been part of you for a long time. It is finally coming home. This is a moment for celebration, not fear. You're going to reclaim this energy using your breath as a guide. Bring the gathered cord to the place it attaches on your body. For example, if it was connected at your belly button, place the wadded up cord there and put your hands over it. If it was attached somewhere that you cannot reach with your hands, use your powerful imagination. You should be getting very good at it by now!

Breath is one of the most powerful tools I have ever found. Take a deep breath in through your nose and then release it through your nose. Do this three more times. Try to have the length of your exhale be equal to that of your inhale. During the inhale, you are creating the power. On the exhale, you create more and more space for the energy of the cord to be reabsorbed into your being. Imagine that with each exhale, the cord becomes lighter and lighter, softer and softer, more and more sparkly. By doing this, you are actually changing the energy in the cord, from dark and heavy to clear and light. After all, you wouldn't want to reabsorb all that negativity. Once it's as light and sparkly as you can make it, imagine that your exhale breaths allow the cord to be absorbed back into your body, into your energy, and into you. Keep up with your breath until you have fully reabsorbed the now-beautiful cord energy back into your body, through all the places where it was attached.

When you've completed reclaiming your energy, take a small break to just sit and relax—but only for a few moments. There is one more big piece to this exercise. The heavy, icky bubble is still sitting there across the room! All that negativity you worked to uncover and release is still hanging around.

7. Release Back to the Universe

Once you've recovered from reclaiming your energy, you will have the extreme pleasure of releasing the old negativity back to the Universe. Walk over to the bubble in your mind's eye. With kindness and love, gently nudge it up into the sky, imagining that you are giving the bubble to your Guides. Ask them to take the bubble, dissolve it into the highest form of light, and send all its energy back to its original home. Imagine seeing the bubble dissolve into light, as all the different energies return to their places of origin. Some of that energy may come back to you— this is a lovely feeling. Some may go back to the other person involved in the situation, and some may return to the situation itself. Just allow it, and receive whichever beautiful light is yours.

Test Your Work

Did this exercise make any changes for you? Is your work moving you closer to your goal? Luckily, you get to test your work immediately. After taking a five-minute break to regroup, it's time to check out what you did. Sit in a comfortable and calm space again and take a moment to recall the memory you worked on, along with the person associated with it. Think about the memory. Does it feel different? Do you feel different? Do you react differently? Does it feel less hurtful? At this point, most people will report that they can't get worked up about the situation the way they could before. It's cleaner. Their emotions are neutral. Some people will feel a little better, but still find themselves emotionally activated. If that's the case for you, it is only a sign that you should go back when you are ready and do more bubble disconnect work around this memory. Perhaps you chose a bigger event to work on, or maybe you released at a slower rate. Whatever result you get, don't judge it as negative—be excited that you were able to affect your energy. You can transform it even more with some additional work.

Creating a neutral response toward this event allows you to make good decisions and learn the lesson from it! When you are able to look back at an event, a relationship with a specific person, or an experience in a lovingly neutral way, you will find that you finally have the strength and the skill to look deeper within it.

The final test to your work is to look back at the situation and the person you chose from your newly objective perspective. What can you learn from this situation, now that you are no longer emotionally activated by it? Are you able to see how your Seed Thought drove you to behave that way? Can you detect the Seed Thought as the underlying driver in the situation? Being able to do this is the result of total clarity—which will lead to the ultimate release you've been looking for. One of my clients, Steve, was finally able to see how his Seed Thought *I'm not good enough* had caused him to leave college before graduating. He no longer blamed his partying roommate—in fact, he saw that he had never believed he would pass his classes in the first place. Realizing this helped Steve understand that all the failures he had suffered were his responsibility—stemming from his Seed

Thought. It took Steve several different bubble disconnects before he was detached enough to gain the perspective on his Seed Thought that he so desperately needed. The understanding he gained shook up the Seed Thought energy so that he could fully release it.

Now that you've started disconnecting from your past, you will find that you're more objective and less emotional about your blocks. If you're not yet feeling significantly less attached to your past in the blocked areas, go back and do the disconnect exercise a few more times. Your readiness to move on to the embodiment step comes from your new ability to look at yourself and your past more objectively, with less emotional activation. That is one of the major factors that allows you to embody the lesson, rather than just intellectually understand it. If you're feeling stronger and more empowered now, you're ready to start embodying the lessons behind your Seed Thoughts!

The Four Stages to Embodiment

There are four major components to embodying the lesson behind your Soul Contracts, rather than just changing your habits. By following these simple steps, you'll reach embodiment much more easily. As with all of the tools this book offers, as you get familiar with the process, you may not need as much structure. For now, follow the steps as I have laid them out. Later, when you have more experience, you can change things around.

Stage One: Tagging

The first stage is called tagging, the act of naming the hidden places where Soul Contracts and Seed Thoughts guide you without your knowledge. If you've been following along, you've unknowingly been tagging already. As you work toward embodiment, you'll seek out those contracts and seeds in the smallest experiences possible. Rather than looking for the obvious places (like how you always feel terrible about yourself whenever your mother visits), start looking for these energies to appear in each moment of your day. Notice if you buy shampoo thinking, *I have to buy the best shampoo because I have the worst hair*. You might walk down the street thinking, *Look at her butt. It's so much better than mine. I just don't have a good butt*. The more minute and inconsequential the moment you tag, the more easily you will eventually embody the lesson.

Once you've found one of these hidden spots, simply say to yourself "Tag! My Seed Thought (or Soul Contract) is showing up right there!" That's all you have to do. The more you do it, the better you get at it. Most people spend only a few days on this piece. Since you have probably discovered that your block touches more areas in your life than you originally thought, it's important to take the time to sleuth it out. The better you get at spotting it, the easier embodiment will be!

If you're still struggling with this, just go back and revisit the awareness step (chapters 6 and 7).

Stage Two: Prediction

At some point in your tagging, you will see your Soul Contracts and Seed Thoughts showing up in a huge number of places. It may be almost funny to see these things rearing their heads in your life. You may even laugh at yourself: the contract completely permeated your life, without you realizing it. Once you have experienced this, you're ready to move into the prediction step, and you will probably naturally begin moving to the next step without intending to. You know that whenever you take certain actions, the Soul Contract or Seed Thought is likely to appear. That is a wonderful thing, because if you can predict it, you can prepare for it; if you can prepare for it, you can change it.

My client Michelle originally thought her block was all about money. As she worked with her Soul System, she learned that her challenge was not limited to money. She also struggled with receiving, being a good person, and believing what she had to offer was valuable. By the time she reached the prediction stage of her Soul System work, Michelle could predict the varied and numerous places where her Soul Contracts and Seed Thoughts might show up. She loved pinpointing each place where the block was about to appear; it made her feel empowered to know it was going to happen. You may find that you enjoy this as well.

Prediction, while simple, is imperative. It shows that you have power over the Soul Contracts and Seed Thoughts, rather than the other way around. When you know the trigger is coming, you can prepare—you can think consciously. When you are being driven by a Soul Contract or Seed Thought to behave a particular way, make the same decisions, or think in a certain way about yourself, you're operating on autopilot. For example, if you have a Soul Contract that says you must sacrifice to prove you're a good person, you will subconsciously decline opportunities for yourself. But if you can predict when that contract or Seed Thought will take hold, you can slow down the process and become more conscious of it.

My client Darcy's Seed Thought *I'm not worthy* and her Soul Contract of poverty drove her to turn down many opportunities to have money in her life. Until she started predicting these influences, she had no sense of power over them.

For the prediction step, just start doing what is probably already coming naturally to you. If you know that whenever you talk to a certain person on the phone, your contract of overgiving shows up, just mention that to yourself. Calling out the contract or seed before it occurs offers you time to prepare yourself—and move on to the next step.

Stage Three: Conscious Decision Making

When you hit your finger with a hammer, your immediate reaction is to yell and move your hand away. Soul Contracts and Seed Thoughts create essentially the same phenomenon. When you encounter a particular situation, you've been conditioned to react a certain way because of your contracts or seeds. With your new power to predict when you will run into that negative situation again, you can make your choice differently.

Imagine that you are building a chair out of wood. Each time you have to work at a certain angle, you hit your finger with the hammer at least twice. Since you know that you tend to misfire at that angle, you decide to be prepared for the next time. Perhaps you have someone else hold the nail; perhaps you get a longer nail. Whatever the solution, you predicted what was coming. Because you knew the outcome, you could take the time to do things differently.

Making different choices, when it comes to your contracts and seeds, works in the same way. But being able to see what is coming doesn't mean you will always alter your decision. In fact, in the beginning, you may only *contemplate* doing things differently. As you improve your forecasting abilities and then your conscious decision-making skills, eventually you'll make a different decision without needing a moment of clarity.

Conscious decision making is not necessarily about always choosing a different action than the one that your Seed Thoughts or Soul Contracts compel you to make—it's about making your decision from a higher vibration. When you decide to close yourself off with a Miniwall Soul Contract that tells you not to let anyone in emotionally, because your Seed Thought says you're not safe, supported, or protected, you are swarming with low-vibrating energies. Conscious decision making helps you make choices before those energies show up. That gap between your prediction of when the energies will show up and the moment they appear is your new conscious decision making space.

Let's look at my client Michelle, who had Soul Contracts around receiving and Seed Thoughts related to believing she was valuable. As she walked into the bank to deposit a check, she noticed that her Soul Contract would usually show up at that time, making it impossible for her to feel gratitude for the payments from her clients. However, once she knew that the Soul Contract was about to materialize, Michelle found herself much less affected by the block. In fact, because she knew it was going to be there, she intentionally (i.e., using conscious decision making) chose the nicest teller in the bank and had a very pleasant conversation with her. The next time Michelle left the bank, she realized that she hadn't gone into panic mode around the money. She made a conscious decision about how to handle the upcoming Soul Contract.

Prediction allows for a pause that gives you a moment of clarity. Now you can decide what is truly best for you, rather than just going with what your contract tells you.

For example, if you would normally volunteer to take your friend's grandma to the grocery store so your friend can stay home and watch football, you'll soon find that there is a small pause just before you give your answer. You're *aware* that this is where your contract would normally show up. Take a moment to ask yourself, "What works for the greatest and highest good here?" Do you have time to take your friend's grandma shopping? Does it put you out? Do you actually *want* to take her? It doesn't matter if you end up making the same decision as usual or a different one. What matters is that the decision comes from a higher-vibrating space, rather than from a reaction to your Seed Thoughts or Soul Contracts.

As you pause to consciously make a decision, you are creating small moments of success against your seeds and contracts. That means you are slowly retraining yourself to have experiences different from what your seeds and contracts have thus far dictated to you. The more of these little successes you have, the easier full embodiment will be!

Stage Four: Full Embodiment

Finally experiencing change in your life and making new decisions is exhilarating. Continue making conscious decisions and keep an eye out for even the smallest successes. In this work, you build and reprogram yourself based on those tiny changes.

To achieve full embodiment of the lesson, you have to move at a sustainable pace. Do not expect to immediately begin telling your brother you won't watch his kids anymore when you've been doing it for the past four years. If you're starting there, you're starting too big. You're not following the steps! If you're trying to move too fast or working on experiences with a heavy emotional load, just go back to tagging. Remember—it's all about teeny-tiny events! As you move from creating minisuccesses to medium-sized successes, remember to celebrate! Build as you grow!

The second level in your work is energetic. Each time you predict one of your Soul Contracts is coming—and you pause, consider, and then make a new choice—you are loosening the energy. You're moving closer to mastering and releasing it. Remember my example of the jar full of sand? Embodying the energy is the ultimate shakeup of those old Soul Contracts and Seed Thoughts! When the energy is shaken up enough, and you're really working with the lesson, it's time to do some energetic work around releasing.

Each success contributes greatly to your embodiment. Sometimes the success comes from making the *same* decision you would normally make—but taking the time to contemplate whether it is for the greatest and highest good. You are beginning to make decisions that come from a conscious place rather than a place of lack or fear. Your choices come from practicality rather than need.

Stage four is about embodying the lesson behind your Soul Contracts. What does embodying really mean in this case? Well, there is a big difference between embodying something at the Soul level and changing a superficial habit. For you to fully embody the lesson, you will have to initiate change at the Soul level. There is no way you can cheat. There is a big difference between information gathering and actual understanding and embodiment of that information and how it affects your life.

Let's look at Johnny as an example. Johnny has been working on his Soul System. He has learned that he eats compulsively whenever he feels intellectually challenged; he knows that he has several Soul Contracts in place that protect him from the Seed Thought *I am not smart*. He has also realized that the lesson these Soul Contracts are forcing him to work on is valuing himself and his intellect. But he only *knows* the lesson; he does not yet believe it.

In doing this work, Johnny has eliminated all the food he typically binges on—everything ranging from grains (breads, pasta, and
crackers) to sweets. He has also made the decision not to go out
to eat for the time being. To the casual observer, it may seem that
Johnny has mastered the lesson because he is no longer bingeing.
The problem is, however, that the only reason he is not bingeing on
food is because he is avoiding temptation. It's a step in the right
direction, but when Johnny truly embodies the lesson, the desire to
binge will be manageable, and he will be able to be around his trigger
foods more easily. In other words, Johnny has changed his habits but
hasn't mastered his Soul Contracts.

In this case, Johnny stopped short of the work he needed to do.
He paused at habit change, rather than continuing on to embodiment. Most people work to change their habits first; as the new
behavior becomes ingrained, they begin to embody the lesson.
Changing your habits is part of the lesson, but not the same thing as
embodying the lesson.

Another way I can tell if someone really has embodied their lesson is through what they say to me. I know that true embodiment
has not yet happened when I hear, "Yes! I've done it, Danielle! I've
embodied that lesson and I'm done. Though I still feel badly about
something else . . ." If you continue to experience a fear or a negative
emotion related to the lesson, it is a sure sign that you have not actually embodied it yet.

When you are fully attuned to that lesson, you will no longer feel
guilty for speaking up, becoming independent, taking care of yourself, or being successful—whatever your embodiment brings. You
will understand and align with your brilliance. You will finally com-
prehend that whatever is for your greatest and highest good is also

for everyone else's greatest and highest good, whether that's immediately clear or not.

The last, most obvious way to tell whether or not you have truly embodied the lesson behind your blocks is to look at your life. Do you see shifts occurring? Are your friends behaving differently or commenting on how your behavior has changed? Are you making more money? Are you on your way to accomplishing a goal you've pursued for years? The Universe needs some time to arrange everything around you to match your new vibration; when it does, you'll know it. Keep looking for your success, and use it as a measure of the work you've done so far.

EXERCISE: FIND YOUR SUCCESSES

Once you feel that you have fully embodied the lesson and cleared the resulting Soul Contracts, it's time to begin finding your successes. These are the result of the work you've done. At first, the changes in your life will begin in extremely small ways. Your job is to find them. If your Seed Thoughts and Soul Contracts made it difficult for you to complete tasks, for example, notice any small projects or errands that you finish now. If your Seed Thoughts and Soul Contracts made it difficult for you to stand up for yourself, keep an eye on your behavior for even the smallest no that leaves your lips. The change could be anything from not buying the cheapest brand, to not allowing someone to cut in front of you in the grocery line. Each small success clears the way for bigger successes. Don't fool yourself into thinking that by the time you get to the embodiment step, you're in the clear or that all your Soul Contracts are gone. You have to make the changes a part of your everyday life.

As you notice each little success, record it. Most people find that carrying a reporter's notebook allows for the easiest recording; you can also use a note-taking app. Recording your success has two purposes. First, if you ever have a down day and feel that you aren't getting anywhere, see-ing a written record of your achievements can be very uplifting. Second, you'll notice a very exciting trend in the notebook. Each success gives you more strength and belief in yourself. You do more each time. You'll take all this strength with you when you move on to mastering your Soul System.

9

Step 4: Mastery

After you have experienced enough moments of clarity through your small and medium successes, you'll naturally begin moving into mastery. You'll know you've reached the mastery phase when you no longer have to keep a tight rein on your behavior regarding your contracts or seeds—basically, things seem to get a little easier.

What does it feel like to reach the mastery step? Keep in mind that reaching this step doesn't mean that you're "fixed." Remember, you were never broken in the first place. This step indicates that you have passed through the toughest phases, and now you're beginning to see results. Often, when someone moves into mastery, their perspective is in flux. They're probably changing how they view themselves and how they fit into the world. They are often less self-critical and more supportive in the areas where they were blocked. They find that just going through the day feels different, if not easier.

People who are working on the mastery step are sitting in a tsunami of emotion. The turbulence is caused by old ways, thoughts, behaviors, and reactions coming into contact with new ones. It is really about the past and future coming together to help you create a new way—but those realizations don't come easily. Habits can be difficult to change, even when the Soul-level energies that created them are released. In this phase, you are breaking up with your old self in favor of your upgraded self. This doesn't mean you're shunning your old self—you are thanking that person for all that you have learned. As we know, there is a lesson in each and every relationship in your life. Now you are free to embrace your brilliant self.

As you continue to grow and keep documenting your successes, you'll also notice that old aspects of your life that used to be important fall away. By the time most people finally reach the mastery phase, their lives look nothing like they did at the beginning of the work. While this may seem scary at the outset, it really is a good thing.

When my client Lisa finally came into the mastery phase, she was working on contracts around settling for things that weren't amazing, not speaking up, and not believing that she was worthy of receiving love without having to earn it. She said to me, "I can't believe how weird I feel. Everything is different. I speak up all the time about what I really want. I'm hit by waves of emotion as I finally let myself see who I am. And I just sit with it. I'm not running around trying to fix everything or trying to convince everyone to go along with what I am doing. I have so much to offer the world! But when those waves of emotion come, they overpower me. I have to pick myself back up and remind myself who I am. I can't believe I get to be this person! I can't believe this is really who I am!"

But this change, as you experience it, often causes strife as well. For example, if you're shifting internally, there must be an outside shift as well. Your environment is going to change. Your relationships, your job, your love life—all of these could potentially be shaken up (and turned inside out) based on the work you've done to rediscover your brilliance. This is why so many people don't want to do this deep work. It's scary to think that your whole world might change when you finally realize who you really are. You'll experience rewards on every level—but it's emotionally, spiritually, energetically, mentally, and physically terrifying to think about what you might lose.

Don't let your fears deter you. Spend your energy peeling away the layers of darkness and negativity that have corroded your life. You are discovering your own divinity, that brilliant part of you that you've left aside for years. Doing the work and reaching the mastery stage will allow you to fall in love with yourself, for the first time ever.

Keys to Mastery Success

Now that you're here, you'll need all the support, information, guidance, and assistance you can get to ensure your success. It will be helpful to understand your echoes. We'll also talk about how to avoid creating more Soul Contracts in the future and how to shift your support network as you go through your transformation.

Echo vs. Reality

As your inner change is reflected into your environment, you will experience something called an echo. An echo can be one of the most frustrating parts of doing this Soul-level work; it throws you off your game. It is a reminder of the Root Belief System you have been working on. It's a small reminder of your big lesson. You know you've run into an echo when you find yourself saying, "I *thought* I had this lesson mastered—why am I having trouble in that area again?"

When you're working in the mastery phase, you still have some energetic remnants of that Root Belief System. Part of that energy is still vibrating within your energy fields. However, because of the work you have done, and because you are seeing and experiencing changes in that area of your life, your new challenges will only be echoes of the original. Keep in mind, if you're not yet experiencing small successes and changes, and you continue to experience your Soul Contracts and Seed Thoughts in the same manner as before, you're not dealing with echoes; you're still dealing with your original issues. It also means you're not ready for this stage yet.

Echoes only show up when you are already experiencing positive changes. These smaller challenges are energetic reminders of how far you've come. You have already developed the tools for handling them and learned the lessons behind them—so the echo keeps you on your toes. Use those reminders, continue shifting your energy, and keep releasing every remnant and trigger associated with that Soul Contract.

I tell my clients to feel excited when an echo shows up in their life. Echoes are not meant to force you to backtrack or accept old energies into your life; instead, they are there for you to resist and use to create more success in your life. Echoes aren't as difficult as your original challenges for two reasons. First, you've already had successes in this area, so you know how to deal with the issues that are cropping up; second, echoes are only reminders.

However, you can get trapped by an echo's energy. If you go into fear mode when the echo shows up, start worrying that your blocks are coming back, and don't stop to manage these energies—you could find yourself feeling as if you are back at square one. Echoes make most people want to drop back into the drama of their old blocks. Instead of backsliding, remind yourself that echoes only show up when you have made significant progress in mastering your Root Belief System.

When an echo shows up in your life, it's time to step back. Ensure you understand why you're getting a little nudge in the area you've been working on. For example, were you getting a little lax about maintaining your new, upgraded energy? Then pull out your toolbox. Should you call on your Guides? Should you do a field clearing before making any decisions? The echo can help take you to the next level, provided you don't allow it to take you down.

Stop Creating Contracts

In the mastery phase, people often start to worry about creating more Soul Contracts. As you begin to experience life with clearer eyes, you fall into this category as well. But there is nothing to fear. You now know how Soul Contracts operate, so by following a few simple rules, making new ones will be the last thing on your mind. Let's review:

1. Remember that, no matter what, you have unseen, yet very powerful support from your Guides. Rather than making decisions totally on your own about how to handle things in a crisis, ask for information, guidance, and assistance from your Guides. They will be happy to help!

2. Don't make decisions when you are emotionally activated. When you feel sad, guilty, upset, hurt, angry, mad, frustrated, vengeful, afraid, or any other negative emotions, your vibration is lower. When your vibration is lower, you are less connected to your intuition and gut instinct—not to mention to your Guides. In this condition, you'll make decisions that are not based on the greatest

and highest good for everyone involved; you'll do things only to alleviate your negative emotions. Take the time to use one of your tools to calm and clear yourself before taking action.

3. As you've seen, Seed Thoughts are created when you bury an emotion in your Soul. Acknowledge what you are feeling at any given time and work with those feelings, rather than trying to bury them. Being human is not about ignoring or getting relief from negative feelings—it's about uncovering what is beneath them. Your emotions alert you to what lessons you are meant to learn. Since you haven't learned them yet, they are now causing those uncomfortable feelings. When you believe in your divinity, see who you really are, and understand the power of your light, nothing that anyone says or does can diminish you.

That's it! Just following those three simple rules will help you spend this lifetime revealing and mastering your old Soul Contracts, lessons, and Seed Thoughts, rather than creating new ones to decipher. It's about staying clear and grounded, noticing when you are not emotionally centered, and taking the proper action. Your awareness of how these energies work and why they exist puts you light years ahead of most people. Be excited about that!

Infusions

As you continue the mastery step, there is one more exercise that can assist you. Simple energetic infusions can help you feel lighter, maintain your higher vibration, and give you the power to complete your work. As you've moved through the process, your energy fields are looking a little like Swiss cheese. As you released certain energies, they have left holes—holes that want to be filled with any energy that goes floating by. With an energetic infusion, you fill these holes with energies that assist you in your goal of discovering your brilliance within.

EXERCISE: ENERGY INFUSION EXERCISE

1. Set Up Your Environment

To begin, set up your environment in the same manner as you have for our previous exercises. Find a private, calm space where you can be totally present and relaxed.

2. Call On Your Guides

Once again, call on your Guide Team—or simply center yourself, if that fits your belief system better.

3. Open Your Energy

In this step, the intention is to create an opening for your Guides to use as they fill you with higher vibrating energy.

Begin by imagining that there is a closed eye about three inches above you, pointing down. Visualize the eye gently opening until it looks down on your head. If you have trouble with this step, get into little-kid mode. Just using your imagination is all that you need to effectively complete this.

4. Infuse

Next, ask your Guide Team to pour 100 percent Divine Light through the eye, into your head, down your neck, through your shoulders and arms, and throughout your body, all the way to your toes. Imagine that this Divine Light fills your entire body (energetic, physical, emotional, spiritual, and mental) and takes over all the spaces left open when you released the Soul Contract and Seed Thought energies. As you are filled, think of the emotions and energies you want to become part of your life. Think of success and freedom and peace, and any others you desire. As you think of each emotion, your Guides will combine the energy of that emotion with the Divine Light. You will be filled with it.

Don't worry about forgetting an emotion or energy. Your Guides know exactly what would be best to fill you with. If you miss any, they support and fill you with the best energies anyway. However, be sure to fill yourself only with positive energies. Rather than using a negative phrase like, "I don't want to be afraid anymore," say something positive like, "I want to feel safe and protected." Whether you state your desire in the positive or negative, it manifests the words you use. Watch what you say! For example, saying, "I don't want to be alone anymore" will only bring you more aloneness; saying, "I want to be in a wonderful love relationship" will attract that relationship to you. Continue this step until, in your imagination, you see that your entire body is full of beautiful, glowing, sparkly Divine Light.

5. Complete

When you feel that you are totally filled—all the way to the top of your head—thank your Guides. Ask them to stop the flow of the energy down into your body. To many people, this looks like a faucet above your head was turned off. Once the flow has stopped, take a moment to seal the space above your head by imagining the eye closing easily and smoothly. Sit quietly for a few minutes and adjust to the change you and your Guides just made.

As you complete this exercise, you'll probably find that you feel good, positive, tired (in a good way), and yet strangely energized. Since you and your Guides have filled you with Divine Light, you will react in alignment with these very positive energies. And you can do this exercise as often as you would like. The more clearing work you do, the more you'll want to infuse yourself with positive, high-vibrating energies to assist you in feeling good, discovering your brilliance, and mastering your Soul Contracts.

Tweak Your Support Setting

Another way to ensure your success is to become conscious of your environment. Is it working for you at every level? As you spend time in the mastery phase, your physical surroundings must shift to match the change you've made in your energies. Since you have a newfound confidence, an exciting ability to take charge, or whatever you have developed as a result of moving into the mastery phase, your job, partner, friends, or diet may no longer suit you. In this stage, people often find themselves making drastic changes without thinking twice—some of the old pieces of their lives no longer fit.

I've had many clients who came through the process only to realize they no longer wanted to be in their primary relationship—and they finally had the power, strength, and belief in themselves to make that change. I've also watched plenty of people change jobs, sometimes on the spur of the moment! Whatever Root Belief System you are working on, any change will touch your daily life in some way. For example, if you routinely complained to a group of friends about your failure in business, you may find that you have lost the desire to talk to that group. On the flip side, you may find yourself speaking more positively to that group. Either way, your feelings regarding those friends will shift as you truly embody and master the lessons you're working on.

The biggest change that people experience when they reach this step is usually in their support system. Perhaps your support system listened when you complained about your blocks. Perhaps someone in your support system always tried to fix your problems. Perhaps you helped everyone else in your support system, but didn't feel comfortable accepting their help. As you let go of the heavier, denser energies in your fields, the people who were a vibrational match for those energies will either let go as well, or they might fight you as you change.

We're comfortable with what we know, even in an uncomfortable situation. This is why a lot of couples who should no longer be together choose to stay together. Even though they may not be happy, the relationship is what they know. The same is true of your support network. As you shift and begin behaving differently, many of those people will subconsciously revolt. They will do everything in their power to try to get you to behave in your old way again. Your former behavior is what they know and prefer, even though it's not what is healthiest. In fact, the more unhealthy the relationship in the first place, the bigger the stink the person on the receiving end of the new behavior will put up.

In addition to someone resisting your changes, you may want to remove people from your life. When someone reaches the mastery phase, they usually decide that having a strong support system in place is one of the most important criteria for success. To believe that you can achieve that goal, get that job, or add a new relationship into your life, you want people around you who can support you with the core of their being. But now that you want superior support, how do you decide who you can trust, and who will fall short?

EXERCISE: SUPPORT NETWORK CIRCLE DIAGRAM
The circle diagram is a perfect tool for evaluating your current relationships and figuring out whom you can and cannot trust. Having a support network is one of the key components to Soul Contract work. At this

point, you may be saying, "But I don't have many people in my life!" but that's not what the support network is about. It's about looking at who is in your life, figuring out what role they should play, shifting those who can't support your upgraded energy into less important spaces, and finding the spaces where you have room to welcome a new person or a certain vibration. The circle diagram will give you a new perspective on what will really support you as you embrace your mastery.

Create Your Circle Diagram Templates

To begin, get a blank piece of paper. Turn the paper so that it's horizontal. Using a pen (not a pencil—pencils promote self-censorship), place one dot in the center of the paper. Once you have placed your dot, draw six concentric circles around the dot so that the final circle is almost as big as the page. Try to have the circles spaced evenly. Some people find it easier to start by drawing the outermost circle and then drawing each smaller circle inside it, until you end with the dot in the middle.

The labels to put with each circle on the paper are as follows:

- Dot in the middle—Me (yourself)
- Circle #1—Soul Partner
- Circle #2—Soul-Level Friend
- Circle #3—Best Friend
- Circle #4—Friend
- Circle #5—Acquaintance
- Circle #6—No-Man's-Land

Now, make two copies of this page so that you have three identical diagrams. At the top of the first diagram, write "current."

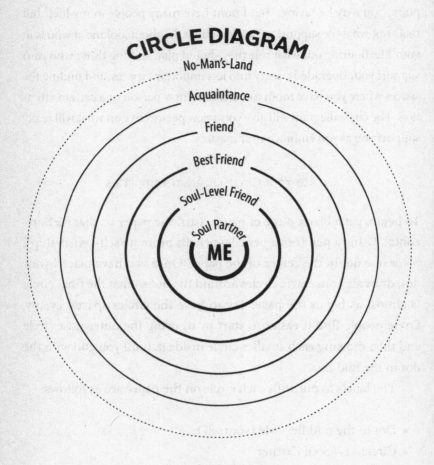

CIRCLE DIAGRAM

No-Man's-Land

Acquaintance

Friend

Best Friend

Soul-Level Friend

Soul Partner

ME

Diagram 4: Circle Diagram

Current Circle Diagram

You are going to map out your friends, family, acquaintances, and so on, on the current diagram. Each person you put on the diagram must be human (no pets) and alive. Don't list someone you pay to have in your life (such as a therapist). Spend some time doing this. You only need to put a dot with the person's name on it near the appropriate circle.

Write in pen to prevent changing your answers around too much—just go with what comes to mind for each person. Figuring out where each person currently sits in your life should be pretty easy. You know who you look to for what. This first part of the exercise will take anywhere from five to fifteen minutes. If you take longer than fifteen minutes, you're taking things too seriously. Get up, walk around, find something to laugh about, and then come back and finish up. Once you have written down everyone you can think of, you can put it aside and move on to the next diagram.

Reality Circle Diagram

For this next piece, we're going to switch things up a bit. For the current diagram, you used my labels. For the reality diagram, you're going to have to use my definitions. You will be going through the same list of people on your current diagram.

Dot in the Middle—Me

This never changes. Your circle diagram is always about you, regardless of which diagram you are working on.

Circle #1—Soul Partner

This is the space reserved for your husband, wife, life partner, Soul Partner—the love of your life. For someone to be in this circle, they must be the person you consider to be your current love partner. (If you don't have a love partner at this time, leave that space open.) Because this is a love partner situation, this person is someone you have sexual feelings about. You should feel comfortable letting them know more about you than anyone else, and you should feel comfortable leaning on them for support. For a person to earn the right to access this circle, it must be virtually impossible for you to be any closer to them. Do not just add your husband because he is your partner. Don't write down the name if you are not actually emotionally close to the person, if you tell your friends things that you can't tell him, if he puts you down or makes you feel badly, or if you are contemplating not being with him anymore. You may have been with your partner for thirty years, but if your relationship is on the rocks, or you don't show your true self to them, they don't belong in that inner circle.

New Definition: Circle #2—Soul-Level Friend

Most people have only one Soul-level friend. This is a person you're almost as close to as your Soul Partner, but it's not a sexual relationship. This is the person who will come over at 3:00 AM because you called them crying about something—and they don't even look at the clock. This is the person who is your biggest supporter, yet can look you in the eye and tell you that something is a bad idea.

New Definition: Circle #3—Best Friend

If you are a social person, you may have two or three best friends. If you are not a social person, this may be the first level of friend that you have. Your best friend knows almost everything about you. They will come to your rescue if you need help and support you in your decisions, even if they don't understand what you are doing. Perhaps you don't share your deepest, darkest fears with this person—but this person has a pretty good idea of what they are. This is someone you can depend on. You have a nice, balanced relationship.

New Definition: Circle #4—Friend

Friends are people with whom you go to dinner or a movie on a week-end. A friend is someone you feel comfortable texting, calling, and hanging out with. You have a nice time with this person; you know a lot about each other, but certainly not all the nitty-gritty details of each other's lives. Most people tend to have more friends in their lives because this type of relationship doesn't involve a lot of vulnerability or risk—it's just pleasant companionship, based on shared interests.

New Definition: Circle #5—Acquaintance

Acquaintances are usually found at work, the gym, or anywhere you go on a more regular basis. This would be someone who knows you are married and have kids or knows what kind of work you do. When they ask, "How are you?" you typically answer, "Fine, thanks." An acquaintance is someone you would not usually text or email. You are not attached in any way to what is going on in their life—if you even happen to know the details.

New Definition: Circle #6—No-Man's-Land

This is the beautiful, energetic space reserved for people who are not part of your life. Usually, this is the area for friends who have drifted away. Ex-husbands and ex-wives end up going in this zone if you have no reason to include them in your life. For some people, you may end up exiling them to this space, while others never make it any closer than this circle. Don't think of this circle as a punishment area. Since we're working with boundaries, think of no-man's-land as a space that keeps you safe, secure, and loved because it helps you set up a good boundary.

Now that you have seen my definitions of the various circles, you might want to revise your current circle diagram. Please do! This is exactly what the reality circle diagram is for. Before you jump in, however, here are a few more tips to make this next step as smooth and accurate as possible.

First, as you probably noticed, a lot of your current diagram is based on what you believe a person is capable of, rather than what is actually happening. When you start looking at each person's actual behavior, based on real interactions, you will find that your treatment of the person is based on their potential. Pay very careful attention to this aspect. For example, I've seen many people doing this exercise realize that the person they called their Soul-level friend wasn't actually playing that role.

Additionally, regarding love relationships, many people will put their partner on the circle where they *want* that person to be, rather than paying attention to the everyday details. For example, when I teach circle diagrams in class, I usually have at least one student who will put her boyfriend on a circle that is too close. She really, really wants the relationship to be more serious. But that doesn't mean her wishes match up with reality.

The reality diagram is about gaining perspective on where people belong in your life, based on their everyday relationships with you—rather than the ideas you've had about them for years. A person's place in your circles is not determined by marriage, the length of time you've known each other, how well things have gone over the years, or where you *want* them to be. It should be based on how things really are. Don't worry about revising your diagram—it will probably change around a bit. That's good—those changes will yield some answers for you! This part of the exercise usually takes longer than the first phase. Give yourself fifteen to twenty minutes to complete your new diagram.

Now it's time to learn from your work. Those two pieces of paper contain some really helpful information! As you probably noticed, there is most likely a difference between your current and reality diagrams. This is because many of us don't spend time thinking about our support systems. At some point in the beginning of a relationship, we decide where it looks like that person belongs, and then we treat that person that way. We do this whether or not we placed the person in the right circle and whether or not things have changed over time. Many people don't realize how often their relationships shift. You friend Christine may be going through a divorce; Joe may be retiring. All of these things affect your friend's ability to be present in your friendship. It is not only healthy to shift friends around on your diagram according to their capabilities; it is advisable.

Compare the two diagrams. Most people end up moving people on their circles outward, but there are also many people who fear vulnerability. They keep everyone at a distance. I've seen many women automatically put their husband in the Soul-partner circle, only to realize that he really ought to be in the friend circle. Think carefully about where you initially placed each person and where you moved them once you started to create your reality diagram.

Many people give up really important spots on their inner circles just because they think they are supposed to. Do you really want your inner circles filled with those particular people? Do you believe that the people in your innermost circles can be there for you, as you go through the process of mastering your Soul Contracts—all the ups and downs, hard work, and amazing insights? These are the people you want to feel completely comfortable calling on as you realize a major Soul Contract. Can they handle what you are saying? Will they think you are crazy? Do you have to censor yourself with any of them?

You may have more adjusting to do on your reality diagram. Don't feel guilty for moving people around—you have every right to have the best support system. This Soul Contract work, as well as just plain being alive, is difficult. Why not set yourself up for success?

As you work, put yourself in different imaginary situations. Picture how each person would act. Distinguish between how you would like them to act (or how they would react on their best day) and how they reacted yesterday or today. Spend more time looking between your two diagrams so you can grasp the reality of your support network.

There are plenty of people who get upset with me when I tell them they cannot put a deceased loved one or pets on the diagram, but that would be misunderstanding the support network. We all get assistance from our loved ones who have crossed over, our Guides and angels, and our pets. However, since humans are social beings, we also need other people we can depend on. If you are a loner, you may only ever have one or two people on your entire diagram, but those people have to be incredibly special to earn their spots.

Take note of the circles that are either empty or have very few names on them. Many people do not have a Soul Partner, so that circle should be left blank. At the level of Soul-level friend, as we've defined it here, most people find that they have just one—if they have one at all. Having a balanced network diagram is not about filling every circle with many names. It is about the quality of each name on the circle.

The blank circles tell a story as well. Do you have many people in the friend circle, but no one closer in? This could mean you don't like to let people into your life. Maybe you don't enjoy feeling vulnerable—or perhaps you used to let people in but got burned. Each circle tells a story about your life, how comfortable you feel asking for assistance, how you handle your friends, and what your boundaries are. Give yourself some time to discover your story. Are you scared of intimacy? Do you invite people into your life, even though the friendship is all about them? Do you shut people out? Your two diagrams give you a good feel for what is really going on. Once you have made your final adjustments, you're ready to move on to the creationary circle diagram.

Creationary Circle Diagram

Pull out your reality diagram and get your third sheet of paper. Label it "creationary." The word *creationary* indicates how you would like your support network to work for you. In this diagram, you'll take what you learned about yourself from the first two parts of the exercise and put it into action. You're aware of how your current support network works; now, you're going to decide what you want to create within your network. You will create the ultimate support system for yourself.

On the circles in this diagram, add the people that you feel completely sure of. You *know* you want a certain person in your life in the future, no doubt about it. Add each name to the appropriate circle, even if it's in a different place than where they were on your reality circle. For example, if your friend Beth has noticed that something is off with you and is offering her assistance, you might consider moving her to a closer circle. If Beth is demonstrating her ability to be a better friend, but your fear (or some other negative emotion) has stopped you from allowing the friendship to develop, put her in a new spot on your diagram.

On the flip side, based on what you learned by comparing the last two diagrams, someone you had high hopes for might need to be moved out a circle to two. That's OK. It's not hurtful to anyone. You are not being malicious, abandoning anyone, or being selfish. You are simply assessing the people around you to find your true relationship with them—as well as what the potential in that relationship really is. Don't move Joe to the Soul-level-friend circle or the Soul-partner circle because he's hot. If Joe hasn't demonstrated his ability to deserve access to those circles, you cannot put him there. This is not a wishful-thinking diagram. It is not supposed to represent what we wish from people; it should represent the roles they really play in our lives.

Once you have reorganized the circles on your creationary diagram, it's time to look for available spaces. You are working on finding the balance in your friendships to know who's safe to lean on as you do your Soul Contract work, as well as identifying where you have spaces open for new people to come into your life. As you work on your Soul Contracts and make those deep changes, you'll find you *want* new people in your life. You want friends who can handle (and are attracted to) your new vibration and your outlook.

So spend some time looking for the spaces. Consider each one to be an open-door invitation for someone to come in and play with you. You are sending a beautiful, loving message out to the Universe *just by identifying* these spaces and affirming that you would love the right people to start filling them.

If one of your circles is empty or you would like to fill a certain spot, draw a dotted circle to indicate the spot you would like to have filled. Because this is a creationary diagram—meaning that you will manifest what you have on this piece of paper—you should include on the paper a key that explains what the dotted line means. This sends your message to the Universe in clear terms. Notice that you are not writing, "I would like to fill this with a really fun, tall, blond girlfriend who wants to spend lots of money on me." Instead, you are indicating, via the label, the kind of relationship you want with this new person. The Universe, which always delivers what you've asked for, will fill in the blanks.

When you have a balanced, fully functioning support network, your work becomes infinitely easier. Notice that I used the word *easier* rather than easy. Soul Contract work is not easy, as you have seen—but if you have a loving environment, or even one truly caring friend or partner who understands and sustains you as you grow, shift, and transform, you will not feel so alone while doing it.

Continued Circle Diagram Success

The Universe will now begin coming through for you. What you've created works like a vision board or a manifestation list. It doesn't really matter what you call it; what matters is that you feel really great about what you've written down and that you would be extremely happy to have your support network look like the diagrams you drew. Clear quartz crystals can assist you in making your message a little louder. Just take a clear quartz crystal (not rose quartz) and place it in the center of your creationary diagram. The crystal will act like a radio tower and broadcast to the Universe what you have written down on the paper. The crystal gives a boost to your work in creating balance! You are asking your support system and the Universe to help you.

As you can see, mastery is all about continual balancing. As you lean on your support network, understand the consequences of your actions, and continually keep your eye on your Root Belief System, you will continue to outgrow your old self. The changes in your life and the results of your hard work will astound you and the people around you. As you feel better about yourself and release hidden, long-buried energies, you can finally begin to create the life you've been looking for.

Becoming the Master

Congratulations! You've now made it almost all the way through the entire Soul System. As complicated as it may seem, its essence is those pieces of yourself that you haven't wanted to look at—those parts were creating all the strife and challenge! Now you can easily believe that you are a perfect, whole, brilliant being.

Although it may be hard to hold the vibration of your brilliance all the time, you'll find that the more you align with these energies, the more you will connect with your perfection. It may be that you go through the steps in this book several times, working with Seed Thoughts and Soul Contracts from many different angles—or it may be that you mastered the blocks your first time through. Whatever your process, pat yourself on the back for working at the deepest Soul level. Most people wouldn't go near this stuff with a ten-foot pole!

You've reached an exciting moment in your Soul System work: the final step. By now, you're probably looking at yourself in a new way. You've learned to give yourself a break when you make a mis-step. You love experiencing the beauty of your Soul that you've thus far uncovered. Well, there is more to come! You are finally ready to release these energies from your body, Soul, and Soul System. What a gift! Let's now move into the most rewarding stage—release.

10

Step 5: Release

As you have learned, creating a Lifetime Soul Contract is a two-fold process. First you embedded a Seed Thought and several Discordant Emotions within your Soul. Then you created a Soul Contract to try to stop yourself from experiencing the Seed Thought and its energies. You've also learned that in order to clear yourself of the Soul Contract, you must master its lesson and release that Seed Thought and the Discordant Emotions. Additionally, you've gone through the first four steps in the Soul System process: Setting Your Foundation, Awareness I, Awareness II, and Embodying the Lesson. You've started to experience great change in your life, from how you look at yourself to the quality of your environment. In this chapter, you'll reap even more rewards from all the work you have already done. You'll learn how to release these energies from your Soul System—it's an exciting time!

As you know by now, you cannot release a Seed Thought or a Soul Contract just by identifying it. However, the work you've done thus far has prepared you to release both kinds of energy. As you enter into this step, make sure you understand how your Seed Thoughts and Soul Contracts were affecting you. Have a sense of success as you consider the changes you've made thus far in your life.

Your Seed Thought, as you now know, holds a vibration that reverberates with a particular resonance. Your physical body had to adjust in order to contain your Seed Thought energies. As you work on the release step, you are shaking up these negative energies, so your physical body must adjust again. By the end of the process, many of my clients have unintentionally lost weight or become more physically active and healthy. They intuitively felt a desire to get up, get moving, and create a physical release, such as playing a sport or starting to exercise. One client started a dog-walking business just because she liked being outside and loved animals. I've seen people quit smoking, get drastic haircuts, go for hydrocolonics, and make other sweeping changes. As you move through this step, remember to pay attention to your body as well as your emotions and energy.

You're finally ready to begin releasing the Seed Thoughts! The Seed Thoughts are buried deep within your Soul, so to start releasing, we will use both your energy field and your physical body.

Seed Thought Release

Your Seed Thoughts anchor your Soul Contracts to you. Once you have released the Seed Thoughts, those Soul Contracts are even easier to clear. Since you are finally viewing your past experiences with more objectivity, and you've been working on embodying the lesson behind the Seed Thoughts, the energy connecting your Seed Thoughts to your contracts is loosened.

When you originally created the seeds, you buried their energies deep within your Soul. For this step, imagine that your Soul is located within your core. As each Seed Thought is ready to be released, it shows up in your physical energy field. This tool is like that old carnival game Whac-A-Mole, in which a mechanical mole pops his head up through a board so you can whack it with a rubber mallet; each Seed Thought will appear in your body by pushing, poking, stabbing, or rubbing through your physical body's energy field. Don't worry if you don't understand this right now—it will make more sense as we go on.

Before we go over this technique, I want to address the question of sickness and disease. I am frequently asked if someone's cancer or sickness is the result of a Soul Contract, and I always give the same answer: it could be. I have certainly met clients who have been sick as the result of a Soul Contract. However, that does not mean all sickness comes from them. I experienced sickness for more than four years as the result of a Bump Contract, so I am very aware of what a powerful motivation disease can be!

For some people, Seed energy actually shows up in the area of the disease. For example, a person who has many Seed Thoughts around not being lovable may find those energies lodged in his physical heart. When something like this occurs, it's a clear indicator that the physical problem and the seed are intricately related. Plenty of other Seed Thoughts, however, will not be tied to a specific physical ailment at all—or you may not see the connection until much later in your process.

Since the Seed energies we will be working with may have manifested as a physical illness, you may rely on physical signs of illness (like a frequent runny nose or knee problems). To use this exercise, you do not need to be physically ill or hurt, and you do not have to logically understand why Discordant Emotion showed up in a particular area of your body—although sometimes the answer will be very obvious. You'll also be relying on your intuition and your imagination, since not everyone has physical symptoms that go with their Seed Thoughts. You may find the energy stored in your physical body, or it may not show up at all.

EXERCISE: SEED THOUGHT RELEASE

1. Set Up Your Space

You know how to do this! Get into a comfortable, private place where no one will bother you while you do this work.

2. Call On Your Guide Team

Call on your Guides or simply sit and calm yourself.

3. Set Your Intention

Next, it's time to set a simple intention. You are performing this exercise to release the energies anchoring your Soul Contracts to you. Setting your intention is the perfect way to let your Guides know exactly what you expect of them—without overstepping your bounds and telling them what to do detail by detail (which no one ever likes). Imagine that you are speaking directly with your Guides, angels, or favorite religious figure. Let them know that you want this work to be for your greatest and highest good. Say that you would like to release all Seed energies associated with the Soul Contract you are now working on. Here is a simple example of an intention prayer: "My intention is that all the work my Guides and I do today is for the greatest and highest good of everyone involved. So be it and so it is."

Feel free to make up your own prayer, using your own words. I've given you this one solely as a template.

4. Call Up the Energies to Be Released

As you settle in, make contact with your Guides, and set your intention, take a moment to think about the blocks you've been experiencing. Think about the Seed Thoughts and emotions associated with your contracts. This shouldn't be difficult, since you've spent plenty of time thinking about these things. Take a moment to really get yourself worked up about those blocks. Allow yourself to feel your anger, hurt, and fear, rather than objectively looking at it. *Feeling* is the primary mode for release in this exercise. Be scared or worried—whatever it takes to bring those energies to the forefront. Be angry, if you have to be. Don't say to yourself, "Wow, this situation has made me really angry." Instead, get into the anger and really feel it. If you're not experiencing emotional upset during this step, then you are staying too objective. Don't act like you are recounting a story—get into the story. Feel it. Live it. Breathe it. Stay on this step until you are experiencing the negative emotions that created and also resulted from your block. Only then are you ready for the next step.

5. Find the Seed Thought's Location

Once you are re-experiencing the anger, hurt, pain, sadness, or embarrassment that those Seed Thoughts have created, notice if part of your body is activated. Does your heart beat harder when you think about your block? Does your stomach get upset? Do you start scratching your ears? Discern what area of your body wakes up when you think about your block. You may be pulled to two or three areas, and that's all right as well. Just take note.

If no particular area speaks to you, use your imagination and get into little-kid mode. Go through the exercise as if you were showing a child what you were doing. What area of your body would you use to explain the block? It isn't important what body part you choose—pick the one that will work best for your imaginary audience, the little kid. That area is now your area for work. You may be very surprised what comes up later.

If more than one area of your body was activated, choose the area that you felt most strongly about. If none of your feelings were very strong, pick the strongest. For many people, figuring out your blocked area is probably a new experience—but that shouldn't stop you from getting accurate information! Avoid analyzing what area "should" be feeling painful, and let yourself be guided to the place you need to go. Remember, if you feel really stuck, just think like a little kid. Often, when you let go and allow yourself to imagine something (or make it up in your head), it allows your Guides to give you the information you need. So, you're not really making it up, even though you think you are. Your Guides will point you in the right direction.

6. Get to Know Your Seed Thought Attachment

Concentrate on the energy in the area of your body that you chose. Imagine what that energy looks like. Is it prickly? Purple? Hot? Cold? Do this, even if you feel like you're making it up. Take a look at the energy—is it only present in one area or does it spread? Is there a particular taste or smell that you associate with that energy? Does it disgust you? Is there slime or motor grease on it?

Spend a few minutes observing the energy that showed up when you consciously brought forth your Seed Thought. Don't worry about what is appropriate or how it "should" look or feel. None of that matters. What is important is that you allow yourself to be completely free, using your imagination to identify this energy within your body. Be sure to take note of the borders as well. Does the energy have fuzzy or defined borders? Is it in a clearly contained shape, or is it hard to define? Once you can clearly and easily describe what this energy is like, you are ready to move on to the next step.

7. Ask Your Guides for Help

It's time to ask for energetic assistance. In this step, your purpose is to turn the work over to your Guides and let them pull out that Seed energy attached to your Soul. At this point, you know what it looks and feels like, so this step will be easy—as long as you can remain in a playful mindset. You're turning this over to your Guides because they know more than you do.

You are stuck in a human body, with your ego and experiences limited to your personal point of view. Your Guides, on the other hand, see the big picture. They are omnipotent, infinitely more intelligent than you. Turning the control over to your Guides also shows your willingness to trust in the Higher Power. Many people try to do all their work—energetic, physical, emotional, mental, or spiritual—themselves. They forget that their Guides want to help. In this step, we're going to practice doing that.

To relinquish the work to your Guides, you simply need to tell them, "Guides, I'm now relying on you to remove the Seed Thought energies I'm ready to release." This is a temporary situation in which your Guides come to the forefront in the process. They are playing the main role and you're in the background. But that doesn't mean your part is less important, and it certainly doesn't mean you aren't aware or in control of what is happening. Remember to maintain your playful, childlike energy; otherwise, you'll block your Guides from this work. Keep your eye on what they are doing as they begin to pull that Seed energy out of your body.

Picture the entire scenario in your head. If you can't see it, use your imagination; it opens up your intuitive abilities and will allow you to more easily picture what is going on. You could even imagine that you are describing the release to someone else. In your head, you might say, "The Guides are going in with a big energetic shovel. They are shoveling out the blackened energy that was hiding under my belly button." Accept whatever comes to mind via your imagination. Do not judge it. In fact, you may want to laugh about it. Be in awe of it!

As you watch your Guides remove the energies, there is one more important thing: the trash. When you are finished with Seed energy (your Guides have removed it completely from your body), it is respectful and important to return it to its rightful space. Imagine that each bit of removed Seed energy is dissolving into the highest form of love and light, whatever that looks like for you. Perhaps you watch the dark energy pulled from your body. Maybe it sparkles into light or looks like a melting ice cube or a computer graphic. This is your process, so open your imagination to anything you can think of.

Once the energy has dissolved into the Light, imagine your Guides directing it back to its rightful home. Some of it may return to you; some may move on to another person or a different place. Where the dissolved energy goes has no bearing on the process. Don't worry about whether it was deep enough or completely effective. Your task at this point is to request that your Guides dissolve the energy and return it home. Otherwise, that heavy, negative energy will hang out in the room where you released it, looking for other dark vibrations to attach to. Wouldn't you rather clear it and send it home?

At this point, you are feeling pretty confident. You're allowing your Guides to release these buried energies from your body. At the same time, you're probably also feeling pretty goofy about making this stuff up in your head. If you are feeling awkward, it's often a sign that you are right on! Most people feel awkward when they do this work because it often feels like you're just making stuff up in your head. Even me!

Continue until your imagination tells you that your Guides have removed all the Seed energies that they could. The energy clean-up correlates directly with all work you've already done around your contracts and Seed Thoughts. It will probably take several tries for all of the energy to be completely released. It may be that you have to go back and work in a new area of the Root Belief System. Where you work in your body, how much effort it takes, and how many energies are released depends on you. Humans are good at hiding emotions, so don't be surprised if you find yourself working on the same Root Belief System in different areas of your body. You worked hard to find special, hidden places to bury your Seed energies! You may have to work just as hard to uncover and uproot them.

8. Check Your Work

You're almost done. Now it's time to check your work. Before standing up, take a few deep breaths and notice how you feel. If the energy was buried in your chest, how does it feel when you inhale or exhale? If it was in your abdomen, do you notice a shift? The first time you do this, you may not notice much of a change; but as you do this several times, focusing on the areas that needed your Guides' attention, you'll find that your physical body will change in ways that you didn't expect. The area will feel different in some way. Perhaps it will feel lighter, more expansive, clearer, or brighter. Any subtle shift in your body is an indicator that you've made some wonderful changes.

Also, notice your emotions. Even though this exercise doesn't directly address your feelings, the energies buried inside you directly correspond to your emotions. At the end of a body-clearing session, you'll probably find that you feel lighter and more hopeful. People have also reported feeling more space around their body (or around whatever area their Guides worked on), which makes them happier. Always test your physical body and your emotions at the end of a body-clearing session. This will help you understand what you have accomplished, as well as what work you want to do in the future.

9. Fill with Light

At the end of this process, it's important to ask your Guides to fill your body with the highest vibration of light. The release of the Seed Thought energy leaves energetic openings within your energy fields. Rather than allowing available energy to fill those openings, you'll feel much better about the work you did if you ask your Guides to fill you with the most beautiful light available.

Remember the infusions technique from chapter 9. You opened a large eye above your head and asked your Guides to fill you with 100 percent Divine Light. Do the same thing now. Concentrate on holding the eye open gently, until you feel, sense, and believe that you are completely full of Divine Light, in every part of your physical body.

10. Thank Your Guides

Finally, after testing yourself, offer thanks to your Guides. They love to feel your gratitude in any way you express it. Also, they have probably been waiting years—or even lifetimes—to help remove these energies from your physical body and your energy bodies, so they will be pretty excited to hear what you have to say.

After you finish the body-clearing exercise, you may find that you feel happier and more intuitive, and your body moves more easily. If your physical symptoms return a few days later, it is a sign to go back and do more body-clearing work. In addition, you will need to continue practicing the embodiment step.

Murky Swamp of the Soul

As you go through this process—working with the energetic tools, loosening old energy, looking at your life with a neutral perspective, and opening yourself at the Soul level—you may encounter a time when you feel completely different. You may feel off or insecure in a way you never have before. In fact, you may even feel like you have gone backward. This is because, in order to release your Seed Thoughts, you pulled up energies that were hidden deep within you for years—or perhaps even lifetimes. These are emotions and energies that you felt were too much, too strong, or too difficult for you to experience at first; when you start engaging with them, you will have to re-experience them, possibly for the first time.

I am always amazed by this part of the process and how people experience it. Most people will face smaller versions of the Discordant Emotions that they buried within their Soul when they created their Seed Thought. I remember one client whose parents had sexually and physically abused her from the ages of three to six. She finally tapped into those memories during the Seed Thought release.

"I just want to be loved! I just want someone to hug me! I feel so alone!" she said, as she sobbed uncontrollably. Her voice was high, and I immediately envisioned her as a little blond girl with pigtails, standing in her bedroom and feeling total despair. She soon came to understand that her temporary discomfort was actually the release of those Seed Thoughts and the accompanying Discordant Emotions. She wasn't telling me in an objective way about what her childhood was like; she was finally allowing herself to have her own experience of her childhood. By doing that, she was physically, emotionally, mentally, and energetically releasing the Seed energies that had plagued her for years.

I call this part of the process "the murky swamp of the Soul." It can last a couple of days or longer. I have been through several murky swamps, where I finally accessed long-hidden energies and seeds. One particular murky-swamp period lasted an entire month! I was resisting tapping into that deep level where my old energy was buried.

Your experience could be much shorter than mine. It depends on whether you have ever worked at the Soul level before, how committed you are, and what pace you can sustain at that deep level. If you try to rush the process to avoid discomfort, you might accidentally push yourself from working deeply at the Soul level to making superficial habit changes. Letting things shift at their own pace will serve you best.

The murky swamp isn't a fun place to be, which is why so many people don't want to work deeply. There is no quick fix. The murky swamp gives you time to align with the lesson and adjust to the changes you are making. One of my clients, Cassie, was emotionally abandoned by both her parents when she was young. In turn, she created the *I'm not good enough* and the *I'm not lovable* Seed Thoughts within her Soul. Her resulting Soul Contract—that she had to take control of everything in her life in order to prove her value—made her very successful in her career but prevented her from being able to experience vulnerability. When she went into her murky-swamp period (which lasted about ten days) she said to me, "But, Danielle, what's the next step?"

She asked me this over and over. She was looking for something to hold on to and trying to find a way to feel in control again. For Cassie, the murky swamp was about learning that there could be safety in not controlling everything. She spent ten days feeling like she was falling, with nothing to grab on to. This is just one example of a murky swamp; your own could be very different.

When you start to question who you are, you're not sure what to do next, and the things that typically comfort you are no longer working, you have reached the murky swamp. This period, although very uncomfortable, is actually a wonderful place to reach. Hooray! Perhaps you are releasing feelings of loss or unworthiness. Perhaps you cry all day. I know that this discomfort seems backward, but it actually means you are going in the right direction. You are finally exploring and experiencing feelings that you are getting ready to release. Don't be scared of this—embrace it! You are really reaching into yourself, digging deep, and pulling up the energy you could never reach before.

Soul Contract Release

Now that you have worked on your Soul Lessons and begun releasing the Seed Thoughts at the root of your Soul Contracts, you're ready to learn a technique to release the Soul Contracts. Luckily, because you've started letting go of that energy, this release will be much easier. If you had tried to release a Soul Contract without first releasing the Seed Thought, you would only make a superficial change in your life—just forcing yourself to behave differently. However, because you've done the necessary work, your reward is the final removal of the Soul Contract block. This change will feel wonderful throughout your body and Soul!

To release Seed Thoughts, you worked on the emotional, physical, and energetic levels. Now, to release Soul Contracts, your focus will be on the energetic plane only.

When you are working at the Soul level, you want to involve the Akashic Records. The Akashic Records are an energetic space where every single thought, feeling, emotion, experience, and sensation that you have ever had (in any lifetime) is stored. While this is not an actual physical place, I encourage you to think of the Akashic Records as a huge football stadium filled with manila files—each one containing some aspect of an experience from one of your lifetimes. Those files also store every bit of pain you have hidden from yourself, every Discordant Emotion, every Seed Thought, and every Soul Contract you have ever created.

Your Soul is very smart. It knows that whatever those Akashic Records say is truth. If your Akashic Records contain a piece of data that says, "The only way to receive love is to sacrifice yourself," then your Soul is going to adhere to that. This is how you can end up with contracts from many other lifetimes affecting you in your current life. That old information is driving your behavior, manipulating your decisions, and more—without you having any awareness of its influence. Normally, the Akashic Records work more smoothly than that. It's a structure that allows you to build lessons into it and facilitates your progress toward enlightenment; however, you can also alter the contents. You have most likely rewritten your records many times throughout your many lives. This is not to say that you cannot make a decision other than what your Soul Contracts compel you to make. We all have free will. However, going against the grain is difficult because you have belief systems, supporting energies, and other factors all driving you to fulfill what that Soul Contract says is right.

For this Soul-level clearing exercise, you're going to work within your Akashic Records to start straightening things out. You are not going to be the one who actually enters the records or makes any of the decisions. Your Guides will do it for you. This is to protect you from yourself—there's a big temptation to go through your Akashic Records and remove everything negative, without understanding the reason for its existence in the first place. That would be a disaster! This exercise will also help you to feel and employ the unconditional, loving support offered by your Guides and the Universe. They will take care of you when you turn the responsibility for altering the Akashic Records over to them.

As you begin this technique, please follow all the steps. The technique is most effective when the energies are set up, the Guide Team is called upon, and the work is turned over to them—all in the proper way.

EXERCISE: SOUL CONTRACT RELEASE

1. Set Up Your Environment

The number one priority is that you feel safe and private in your work space. Get comfortable and make sure you won't be disturbed as you begin this exercise.

2. Call On Your Guides

Call on your Guide Team and let them know what you will need. By now, you should be an expert at this!

3. Call On Your Akashic Records Team

Each of your Guides has a specific job. Some of your Guides have been with you since you were conceived. They help you in a general way. You also have Guides who are project based and assist you as you learn a certain lesson or accomplish a particular goal. (For example, I have a Guide Team helping me write this book!) To work through this process, it is especially helpful to engage with the part of your Guide Team specifically devoted to working at the Soul level. This team is called your Akashic Records Team. Now you can invoke your entire Guide Team—which will include your Akashic Records Team. You may wish to use all your Guides, but I've found that most people prefer calling on the specific team for this kind of work.

Everyone has an Akashic Records (AR) Team. In my experience, most people's teams consist of three Guides; however, I've seen teams of ten and teams of one. Don't be discouraged if your team isn't average; this is only a guideline.

Also, it is not important that you see, hear, feel, or sense your AR Team when you call on them. It is only important that you make your prayer request. To call on your AR Team, you can say a simple prayer, such as, "I am now calling on my AR Team to assist me with this work today." Calling on your AR Team not only activates their energy but also sets your intention to work at the Soul level—and that is the most important facet of this particular tool!

4. Set Your Intention

Now, think of what you'd like to accomplish through this work. You are going to release the newly uncovered energy trapped in your Soul Contracts. Setting your intention is the perfect way to let your Guides know exactly what you expect of them without overstepping your bounds and telling them what to do. To set your intention, imagine that you are speaking directly with your Guides or angels. You can use the same intention idea you used when releasing your Seed Thoughts, if that works for you. You could say:

"My intention is that all of the work my Guides of 100 percent Divine Light and I do today will be for the greatest and highest good of everyone involved. So be it and so it is."

Feel free to make up your own prayer as well.

5. Connect to the Light

In order to ensure that you are in the best possible emotional, energetic, mental, and spiritual state, you will need to expand your energy bodies to connect with your intuition and your natural divinity more easily.

Begin by imagining that you are standing with your arms at your sides—or actually do this with your physical body. Imagine that your energy is a beautiful, silver, sparkly column of light. It surrounds your body. It is much taller than you. Now, using your breath, begin to expand this column in all directions around you. With each exhale, imagine the column getting wider and wider. Imagine that you feel more and more space around you. Using your exhale, grow the column until it stretches fifty feet around you in all directions. The column goes behind you as well as beneath your feet. If you forget these areas, you may end up feeling out of balance.

Expanding your natural column of light assists your Guides as they release the energies. Here's how it works: Imagine that you have two glasses. One is an eight-ounce glass and the other is a sixteen-ounce glass. They each hold twenty marbles. Your task is to pick the marbles out of the glasses one at a time. It's going to be easier with the larger one, right? It's the same with the column you've made around your body. Expanded energy creates a feeling of power and strength—and having wider, expansive energy helps your Guides get access to what needs to be released. If you were feeling small and powerless, you would not have the same results. So expand your column! There is no need to go beyond fifty feet. For some people, this may be easy, or it may take some time. Don't worry about that. Just do the work to get your column of light to fifty feet.

6. State the Soul-Level Clearing Prayer

This clearing prayer will be most effective if you say it out loud in a strong and powerful voice. You're letting your Guides know that you *really* want to release these energies! The prayer I've written here is only a guideline. If you feel drawn to make up your own, please do so—and feel free to use mine as a template. Just make sure you hit the same major points and that you clearly turn the work over to your Guide. Say the following prayer out loud:

"I now consciously release all Discordant Emotions, Soul Contracts, and Seed Thoughts of any kind that are no longer serving me. This includes all that my Soul and my Guides know I am finally ready to let go of as well as:

[Take a moment here to talk with your Guides about your situation, the energies you have been working on, and the areas where you would like them to look. Remember, you cannot choose what will be released—but you can let your Guides know you think you are ready.]

"Please release all resulting physical emotional, mental, and spiritual attachments and clear my Akashic records, consciousness, and unconsciousness, and assist me in aligning my vibration with my greatest and highest potential.

"As these energies clear from my being, please gracefully and gently infuse me with the following energies:

[Now, take another moment to think about the emotions and feelings you would like to have in your life. State these emotions only in a positive way. Stick to simple words like *peace* and *excitement*. Imagine these energies entering your body through the top of your head.]

"Thank you, thank you, thank you."

Spiritual attachments are the additional energies you carry as a result of your Soul Contract. In doing this work, you're giving your Guides every opportunity to clear your deepest levels as much as possible; that is why this clearing prayer is written this way. Remember, don't try to manifest specific things. If you leave the details to the Guides, you'll find you're much happier with the outcome!

7. Fill Yourself with Light

At the end of the process, it's important to ask your Guides to fill your body with the highest vibration of light. Releasing the Soul Contract energy leaves energetic openings within your energy fields. (Remember the Whac-A-Mole?) You'll feel much better about the work you did if you ask your Guides to fill you with the most beautiful light available. Use the same technique we covered in earlier exercises. When you feel, sense, or know you have been completely filled, remember to close the eye above your head.

8. Thank Your Guides

Finally, offer a big thank you to your Guides for all their assistance in this work.

No one can predict how your life will change in response to the work that you have done through this book. You are going to undergo some obvious changes—what you would expect—but you will also experience shifts that you didn't see coming. Remain open by continuing to look for small successes. If you can continue to congratulate yourself for any and all progress you make, you will open yourself to experiencing a greater life here on Earth and a greater life within your own skin.

Side Effects

You should know that there are some side effects to the clearing techniques. They are not negative, but you should be aware of them. When you have completed the exercise, pay attention to yourself for the next three to ten days. Most Soul Contract releases take up to ten days to complete. This is because the energies did not all arrive within you at once—you must go through an unwinding process as they leave you, one by one. Additionally, most people can't physically handle an instantaneous clearing. The physical body holds a certain density to house your Soul and all your Soul Contracts. As you release these energies, your physical body will need to adjust as well—most of the time, this means losing physical density.

Additionally, while saying the clearing prayer and for several minutes afterward, many people experience these symptoms:

- Buzzing of hands, head, feet, torso, etc.
- Heat in hands, head, feet, etc.
- Perspiration
- Cold body parts
- Notice a cold or warm breeze in the room
- Feel like they are taller
- Feel like their neck is longer
- It seems to become brighter in the room
- Lightness on their shoulders (like a weight has been lifted)
- Easier breathing
- Swollen hands
- Feeling of happiness or hopefulness
- Eyesight seems more clear
- One or both sinuses open
- Pressure on chest
- Lack of pressure on chest
- Heart palpitations

The list of side effects is long but is not not set in stone. You may not feel anything. You may notice or sense other side effects. Your physical experience of the clearing does not reflect its effectiveness. If you feel nothing, that only means that you subconsciously chose not to feel or sense the energy as it was released. You could have a Soul Contract around that experience, or it could be for some other reason. Either way, it doesn't mean that the clearing didn't work; it means that's how you chose to go through it.

Tips for Success

As you go through the three to ten days following the clearing work, there are several things that you can do to assist in the clearing and to make it as smooth as possible:

1. Drink plenty of water. For each pound that you weigh, drink 60–70 percent an ounce of water per day. This means that if you weigh a hundred pounds, you need to drink sixty to seventy ounces of water every day until the clearing period is complete. Remember that water is flow, and you want your release to flow easily!

2. Go easy on yourself. You may find that you notice yourself tearing up for a moment or getting upset more easily—and the feeling comes from nowhere. Just remind yourself that you're releasing the old, buried energies. This can be a trying time, so don't push yourself very hard.

3. Do things that are fun, out-of-the-ordinary things. Do not sit around at home just saying, "I am clearing" as you obsess over every single thing you do, say, and feel. A watched pot never boils! Having fun, laughing, spending time with friends, and trying new experiences all put you in a positive state of mind that will facilitate a smoother and easier release.

4. Don't worry about what you are releasing. We often tend to get hung up on labels and stories. Instead of telling a friend all about your whole process and the various Soul Contracts you're working on mastering and releasing, do something productive. You could try writing, meditating, or maybe even riding a roller coaster. Becoming attached to one or more specific phrases, such as *I hope I cleared that Soul Contract of poverty* or *I hate that Soul*

Contract of poverty keeps the energy of that contract alive within you, rather than allowing you to release it.

During the clearing, you may find yourself to be slightly more emotional or edgy. Your daily existence might feel more unsettled. You may also find that you want more time alone—or less. Everyone goes through the process differently. Whatever you choose to do, just try not to wait out this period, hoping everything will go back to normal. If you followed the steps, the clearing will boost your desire to master your Root Belief System. This means that things will never go back to your old version of normal—the way you were used to navigating your life. That was something that you developed based on the energy guidance of your Soul Contracts.

Now that you have released those energies, you will not have those Soul Contracts nudging you to behave in certain ways. It may feel weird to you. You may not know who you are—or you may feel off balance. When that odd, neutral feeling overcomes you (usually three to ten days after the clearing work), you will know that the clearing is complete. You are finally ready to start looking for your successes.

It is exciting to move into the releasing step. That feeling of freedom is like no other: the discovery of your brilliance within comes with it. The day you realize that you are not broken is one of the biggest events in your current lifetime. It is the signal that you have learned at least one of your Soul Lessons. You're now ready to move forward to the next level of your human experience. Congratulations on making it this far! The road hasn't been easy—but your Soul left you a trail of breadcrumbs (in the forms of Root Belief Systems and Seed Thoughts) so that you could find your way. Remember to say thank you to your Soul!

You've taken the time to understand your Soul System and learn how it has secretly influenced you for years and years. (Many people go through an entire life without ever learning this information!) Then you sifted through those negative influences and eliminated them by working deeply at the Soul level. What did that process give you? A beautiful, brilliant Soul System that you can access every moment of every day. Now, when trying something new like kayaking or public speaking, you will have a direct line to your divine self, which will show you how brilliant you really are.

A lot of self-love comes with this final stage. Some people enjoy that feeling so much that they want to immediately start working on another Root Belief System. While this is admirable, give yourself a break! Take some time to wake up and feel excited about who you are. Give yourself a few weeks—or even months—to interact with others with your new vibration. Feel strong and confident in your work, noting how your inner power now shines through.

Physical manifestations take a little longer to show up than the emotional ones. So, if you're hoping to bring love, a new job, or whatever you've made room for into your life, give the Universe time to respond. Remember, none of this work is about instant gratification. It's really about the deep, Soul-level changes that are reflected first in your energy, then in your emotions and beliefs, and then out into the world. Take it easy and watch as your world begins to shift.

Then use your brilliance to go back and rediscover more!

Acknowledgments

First, there is no way I could have written this book without the support of my husband, Kevin. You gave me the courage to find myself and to share that person with the rest of the world.

I also could not have written this book without the support of my shining little star, Cole. Cole, you have no fear about being who you are. I am so grateful to be a part of your very special life. I learn something new from you every day.

Since the day we met, John Holland has been my biggest supporter. Thank you for showing me how to do it. Your guidance, love, and kindness mean the world to me.

Pam, I couldn't ask for a better person to put my trust in. Every day, you are there, helping me, keeping me on track, and reminding me of the things I should not forget. I'm so grateful to have you in my life!

Thank you, Cindy Mattingly, for all that you've been for me in my life. I love you and appreciate all of our time together. Thank you for being such a wonderful sounding board!

Monika, thank you for being a dear friend, listening when I needed it and reading through my first draft! Thank you.

Kerri, thank you for giving me stability and reminding me to laugh at myself.

Mom, you are an outstanding teacher. I continue to learn from you every day. Thank you.

Bella, Kelso, Mabel, Dashiell, and Jesus the Chihuahua: thank you for being such powerful guides and teachers, and for continuing to work with me even when I resisted.

Bee, thank you for seeing me as I am and accepting me. It's amazing to learn so much through friendship.

Bob, thank you so much for helping me figure out what I was talking about! Thank you for your linear thinking and heartwarming support.

You were one of the first people to take a chance on me, Cathy Levine. Thank you!

Anna O., thank you for sticking with me even though I wasn't acting like your usual client! Thank you for understanding that it all had to feel right.

Dougall and David, you are such wonderful friends and supporters. I'm so grateful to have you in my life every day!

A. J. Baime, you're the one who made me realize that I could do this. Your success helped me go further. Thank you.

And thank you to the people who showed me how strong I could be by believing in me, each in their own way: Joy Costanza, Tara Holden, Laura McGourty, Leigh Hefferon, Terry Nolan, John Burgos, Julie Stockbridge, Colette Baron-Reid, Debbie Calderon, Michelle Broussard Moseley, Cindy Kubika, Michelle Skaletski-Boyd, Bruce Butcher, Nancy Santopietro, and Carol Donohoe.

Frequently Asked Questions

I answer many of these questions throughout this book, as well as on my website, on my Facebook page, and in my classes. I've compiled a list of some of the most popular Soul Contract questions for you here!

Why did you call them Soul Contracts?

The Soul Contract energies I talk about in this book are energies that are much more intense than just a bad habit. They have adhered to you at the deepest possible level, which is the level of the Soul. They are also binding energies. Once you've taken them on, you cannot simply decide, "OK, I'm done with these!" and be done with it. You must go through a process to learn the lesson behind them before you can release them. They are binding in the same manner as a legal contract.

How are the Soul Contracts you're talking about in this book
different from the Soul Contracts I already know about?

Most people think of a Soul Contract as a binding agreement between
a person and their Soul Mate. The Soul Contracts in this book also
relate to your contracts with others, but more importantly, to the
contacts you have made with yourself.

Are my Soul Contracts predestined?

You have Soul Contracts because of the Soul Lessons that your Soul
determined you need to learn during this lifetime; however, which
Soul Contracts you choose along the way to help you learn these
lessons are not predetermined. Instead, your contracts are based on
your particular reactions to your experiences and emotions.

How do I avoid making more Soul Contracts?

The simple answer: Concentrate on keeping yourself clear, calm, and
grounded. Focus on having a solid foundation. Remember to call on
and trust in your Guide Team for guidance along the way. Do not
make decisions when you are in an activated, emotional state, if you
can help it; this will help you stay connected to your intuition as you
make decisions for your greatest and highest good. This concept is
also discussed in depth in the mastery step (see chapter 9).

Does anyone have no Soul Contracts at all?

Soul Contracts represent areas that we need to work on to evolve
spiritually. When someone has mastered all of their Soul Lessons,

they will, of course, have no more Soul Contracts and no more need to evolve. In other words, someone without any Soul Contracts will have done all their spiritual work, and they will have reached the state of enlightenment we're all working toward. This person would no longer need to take part in human lifetimes.

How do you know when you are done with a Soul Contract or a Root Belief System?

The effects of mastering a Soul Contract or Root Belief System manifest in both your inner being and your external environment. You may feel better, have more confidence, feel happier, or speak up more; you may also get the job you wanted, experience unconditional love, or find the support you have been looking for. Completion is about learning, mastering, and then allowing your energy fields to shift. As that occurs inside you, your world will reflect it.

Does it take both people to dissolve a Soul Contract?

Mastering your Soul Contract with another person doesn't require your partner to master their end as well. Your completion is not dependent on their completion and vice versa. For more details, check out the section on Pre-Birth Soul Contracts (see chapter 2).

Do we have different contracts with the same Souls, but in different lives?

Our Souls reincarnate in Soul groups. This means that in each lifetime, you will experience life with the same Souls. Since many Soul Contracts are pre-birth agreements, you will create Soul Contracts with the same Souls—however, the contracts themselves may be very different. If you don't complete a Soul Contract in one life, it doesn't mean you must have that same Soul Contract with the same partner Soul in another life. Pre-Birth Soul Contracts are intended to help you learn. If the agreement didn't work in one life, your Soul will find another way to help you learn that lesson in the next life.

Can I have a Soul Contract with my pet?

You have a Soul Contract with every animal you've ever come into contact with. And what's even more exciting is that the Soul Contracts with your pets will support the Lifetime Soul Contracts that you're already working on! It's like everything and everyone is conspiring to help you live and feel the best you possibly can.

How do my Soul Contracts affect the people around me?

You're probably already becoming aware that your Soul Contracts and Seed Thoughts affect your relationships. For example, someone who constantly overgives will create relationships in which they are always expected to overgive. I have never met anyone whose relationships were not formed and continually touched by their Soul Contracts. It is impossible, as you will see, to choose a friend, a lover, or even a boss without having your Soul System guide that choice. This is why it is so important to have a healthy Soul System.

Will all my relationships change as I work on my Soul Contracts?

Yes, all your relationships will change as you work on your Soul Contracts and Seed Thoughts. This is not because you are intentionally changing your relationships, but because approaching yourself and your life from a new vantage point will cause all your relationships to evolve. Some will break apart, while others will become more bonded and deeper. In the long run, all these relationship changes are for your, as well as everyone else's, greatest and highest good.

Can you have more than one Seed Thought in your Root Belief System?

Yes. Seed Thoughts often appear in twos or threes. For example, someone whose seed says *I'm unsafe or unsupported* might also have a seed that says *I'm not worthy*. We tend to be very thorough when we create our Seed Thoughts! Luckily, as you work on one Seed Thought, it often addresses the other seeds in the Root Belief System.

Is it a Seed Thought or Soul Contract that is challenging me?

It's actually very easy to figure out what you are dealing with. A Seed Thought is a deeply held, Soul-level, negative belief that you have about yourself, while a Soul Contract is a deal you make with your-self in order to avoid experiencing that belief. If the energy you're looking at is more of an action ("I must stay invisible" or "I must not speak up"), you're looking at a Soul Contract. If the energy you've identified is a belief or an idea about yourself (such as *I'm not good* or *I'm a failure*), then it is a Seed Thought that is challenging you.

What does it mean to master a Soul Contract?

When you master a Soul Contract, it means you have understood and learned the lesson from your Seed Thoughts and subsequently released the seeds, the contract, and the Root Belief System.

What happens when I release my current Soul Contracts?

People who have mastered their Soul Contracts and Seed Thoughts get to experience a new level of living. Those who struggled with Soul Contracts of not feeling supported and protected in their lives will often experience a huge increase in the support and abundance around them. For example, that could mean making new friends, finding the love of their life, making more money, or receiving acclaim for a job well done. What you experience as a result of your work will be different from what others experience, because the results are completely dependent on the work of each individual.

After mastering a Soul Contract, how do you prevent
the fear of repeating the same lesson?

If you have a fear of making the same mistake, then you haven't really mastered the contract. Mastery is true command—it's not just understanding the lesson. It's *getting* the lesson and embodying it. When you have embodied all that you've learned, there will be no fear about repeating a challenge or making the same mistake. Additionally, you don't beat yourself up if you make a choice following your old pattern rather than the new one.

When I have difficulty working with my Soul Contracts, how do I
keep from second-guessing everything that I am doing?

If you're not making any headway on your Root Belief System, it's time to step back and look at what might be getting in the way. Perhaps you should address a different Root Belief System first. Trusting yourself, believing that you can make good decisions, and relying on your intuition are good places to begin working. Once you've mastered that part, you'll be able to move on to your other stuff.

What if I break the wrong Soul Contract?

Because of the way that Soul Contracts work, it is impossible to break the wrong one. In fact, it's a foolproof system! All Soul Contracts are there for you to learn from. Trust that the things bothering you the most right now (the Soul Contract blocks) are surfacing because the time is right for you to understand, master, and release them.

Can a Soul Contract be the cause of an illness?

Yes. This is a Bump Contract, but not all sickness is caused by Bump Contracts. Some Seed energy manifests directly in a related body part, but many will not be tied to an ailment at all. This is covered in depth in the chapter on alternative Soul Contracts (see chapter 2).

Can a challenge be comprised of multiple contracts?

Yes. Getting through this involves identifying several Root Belief Systems. Identifying these will be the key to your success in Soul Contract work, although it is not necessary to identify all of them at once—just begin with the most overwhelming or negative, and the rest will follow. Trust your Guide Team and the Universe to reveal each contract at the appropriate time.

What happens if I give up because the contract is too hard?

When you stop addressing a particular Soul Contract or Root Belief System, the world doesn't wait for you to get your motivation back.

In fact, the challenges caused by those contracts will not only continue—they will grow bigger and bigger until you finally give in and go back to working on them.

What will happen if I don't want to work on my Soul Contracts?

I've met people who wanted to know what their Soul Contracts were, but were not ready to work on them. I've also encountered people who only wanted to work on their Soul Contracts in a superficial way. And then, of course, I've seen many people who didn't want to know anything about their Soul Contracts at all; they just wanted their inner pain to end. All of these people's systems will only get bigger, harder, and more challenging. For example, if you ignore the fact that you feel afraid to speak up, you'll run into bigger and bigger issues with more and more dire consequences until you finally address your fear of speaking up. This is not a punishment—it's simply a big signal. It's easy to ignore a small signal, but when something is flashing in your eyes and blaring over a loudspeaker, you're eventually going to get fed up and address it.

Are there Soul Contracts that only exist to teach me to be happy?

Yes. You might have created a Soul Contract to help you see that you can be happy, you deserve to be happy, and that being happy is not selfish. There are many Soul Contracts around being happy.

When I have a Soul Contract with another person (a Pre-Birth Soul Contract), will I always feel uncomfortable with that person, or can I feel completely at ease with them?

How you feel regarding that person depends on what you are supposed to learn from them. Perhaps you're supposed to learn how to be more assertive. This person might put you in situations where you have to stand up for yourself, *or* they might model how to have beautifully clear boundaries, so that you learn by observing. Perhaps you are in awe of your friend, and you question whether you will ever learn to stand up for yourself as well as she does. This contract won't manifest as negativity between the two of you—but you might still feel insecure. Your discomfort is a sign of your growth.

Is there any particular ceremony for destroying my Soul Contracts?

Many clearing rituals—such as burning parchment paper with the contracts written on them—claim to clear Soul Contracts. Rituals work because the person doing the ceremony did all the emotional and energetic work leading up to it and mastered the accompanying energies. In other words, the ritual is a meaningful marker for the end of a lesson—but without the inner work (as I've described in this book), the ritual is not effective. You must master the lesson.

Should I continue a not-so-healthy relationship to prove that I can love unconditionally or move on to prove my worthiness?

Mastering your Soul Contracts is the way to your greatest and highest good. Staying in a not-so-healthy relationship to prove you can love unconditionally would mean not loving *yourself* unconditionally. You're not acting for your own greatest and highest good. When you make choices for your own greatest and highest good, it is for the greatest and highest good of all. Additionally, Soul Contracts cause you to feel like you must prove something. When you discover the emotions and energy underlying those Soul Contracts, you'll realize that you don't have anything to prove to anyone. You are your light, no matter what.

> Do I need to know who I was in a past life in order
> to work on my contracts? Should I do a past-life regression
> before doing this work?

Although some Soul Contracts and Seed Thoughts are formed in past lives, it is not necessary to delve into or even believe in past lives to do this work. We live in the now, so let's work in the now and address the current challenges, Seed Thoughts, and Soul Contracts.

> Will this book bring me a greater understanding of my purpose?

This is such a popular question! The answer is, indirectly, yes, but directly, no. The point in doing this work is to clear out the energies that are standing in the way of your feeling clear, competent, good, whole, valuable, pure, supported, and so on. As you release these energies, you will feel more confident and more able to act on the intuitive urges guiding you to your purpose for being.

Glossary

Animal Soul Contract—Animal Soul Contracts are Soul Contracts that are identical to Relationship Soul Contracts, except that they occur between a human Soul and an animal Soul instead of occurring between two human Souls.

Bump Contract—This type of contract is a pre-birth contingency plan put in place by your Soul. If you are struggling to learn one of your Soul Lessons, a bump will show up in your life to nudge you back toward that lesson.

Discordant Emotions—These are the intensely negative emotions you were feeling at the time you embedded your Seed Thought within your Soul. These emotions are embedded with your Seed Thought, which is why you continue to re-experience them as an adult until you release them.

Guide Team or Support Team—These are the energetic beings that assist you every day in your life. They are also called your Spiritual Guides.

Lifetime Soul Contract—This is a contract that you made in either your current existence or a past lifetime. It was formed as a response to your negative reaction to a Seed Thought (or Thoughts) when you tried to take control of your life.

Light Calls—Light Calls are the reprogramming phrases that you say out loud to help upgrade your energetic support and align with the Light.

Miniwall Soul Contract—This is a very common Soul Contract. A person with a Miniwall will resist making deep friendships. Instead, most people with a Miniwall will assist others who need help, while never letting anyone into their own heart.

Past- and Present-Life Soul Contracts—These are terms used to describe when a Lifetime Soul Contract was created (either in this current lifetime or a past lifetime).

Pre-Birth—Based on the idea that the Soul reincarnates from one lifetime to another, this is the state of the Soul between two lifetimes when Pre-Birth Soul Contracts are made.

Pre-Birth Soul Contract—This is a Soul Contract that is assumed by your Soul while it is between lives. Pre-Birth Soul Contracts are agreements that are made when your Soul is in the highest possible vibrational state.

Relationship Soul Contract—This is a type of Pre-Birth Soul Contract. It is a pre-birth agreement between two Souls to help each other learn individual Soul Lessons.

Root Belief System—A Root Belief System is comprised of Seed Thoughts and their attached Soul Contracts. In a Soul System, you can have several different Root Belief Systems. The goal of this book is to teach you how to clear your Root Belief Systems by mastering their components.

Seed Thoughts—This is an original thought you had about yourself (usually accompanied by intense negative emotions called Discordant Emotions) that you planted in your Soul, rather than experiencing it and growing.

Soul Contract—A Soul Contract is an energetic bookmark within your Soul. It marks a lesson your Soul needs to learn. When you are not getting the lesson or making progress on it, the Soul Contract can create a block in your life, such as keeping you from finding success or wreaking havoc in your relationships or health.

Soul Lesson—Each person has several Soul Lessons they are meant to learn throughout their lifetime. Each time you learn a Soul Lesson, you are clearing Seed Thoughts and Soul Contracts and moving closer toward claiming your brilliance, finding balance in your life, and attaining true enlightenment.

Soul Purpose—This is the thing you came to do in this lifetime. Whatever your Soul Purpose is, it will assist in the evolution of humanity in some way.

Soul System—Your Soul System is made up of your Soul, your connection to Source and protection by the Universe, unconditional love, and your perception, as well as any Root Belief Systems you have created. The work in this book is based on building a healthy Soul System for yourself.